BLOCK GENIUS

201 pieced quilt blocks with No Math charts

by Sue Voegtlin

Landauer Publishing, an imprint of Fox Chapel Publishing

BLOCK GENIUS

201 pieced quilt blocks with No Math charts

by Sue Voegtlin

Landauer Publishing, *www.landauerpub.com*, is an imprint of Fox Chapel Publishing Company, Inc.

Editor: Doris Brunnette
Art Director: Laurel Albright
Photographer: Sue Voegtlin

Library of Congress Control Number: 2016945803
ISBN: 978-1-935726-90-6

We are always looking for talented authors. To submit an idea,
please send a brief inquiry to acquisitions@foxchapelpublishing.com.

Printed in Singapore

10-9-8-7-6-5-4-3

 FACEBOOK.COM/
LANDAUERPUBLISHING
 YOUTUBE.COM/
LANDAUERPUBLISHING
 PINTEREST.COM/
LANDAUERPUB

Table of Contents

Foreword

When our editorial team talked about doing a block book, I thought, "how hard could that be?" so I volunteered. I'm the staff photographer at Landauer and I'm a bohemian quilter. I am not a perfectionist, I don't like to be tied to rules or told there is only one right way to do something. I make quilts to be used... whether by kids, other loved ones, or even my dogs!

So knowing that about me, I need to explain I am not the "Genius" in the title. The genius is the versatility of the grid format, the 6, 9, and 12-inch blocks, and the math that brings it all together.

We decided the blocks should be traditional and made in sizes used most commonly by quilters. Many of the block designs are nearly 100 years old, some easily recognizable and others begging for recognition. It's amazing to me that things that old can still be important in this age where "newer, faster, and the latest-greatest" seem to be at the top of the list.

As I started to choose blocks, I began taking a closer look at them. Probably 70% of the blocks I made had no instructions so I dissected them to find the components in each block. How did the pieces go together? What shapes made up each block? Could I change the block's construction and still maintain the same design? How much math did I have to re-learn to write instructions? Would I have fun doing this?

From writing instructions, to cutting fabric and sewing each block, the process wasn't fast. For me, this was part of the lure. Slowing down allowed me to improve my accuracy, whether it was cutting, sewing and matching 1/4-inch seams, or pressing. It gave me time to play and experiment with color on a much smaller scale; one block at a time doesn't take much fabric so I wasn't out much if I didn't like the colors I chose.

But, did I have fun? You bet I did! I have a library of over 200, nine-inch quilt blocks neatly tucked into plastic sleeves of three ring binders. They will be my block reference go-to. I have already started a few projects using block patterns from my collection.

I think this book is a great reference tool since *the math is done for you.* I hope it inspires you to sew, slow down, enjoy the process, play with color and create new designs for your own projects.

Sue

Pick a Block...

...any block. Construct it as you see it or change the colors to make it your own. I wrote instructions for the blocks in this book based on the No Math Block Chart, page 142. It's a perfect reference when you decide to make blocks you don't find here, or if you are ready to design your own. Step out of the box! Color outside the lines! Create your own beautiful blocks!

BLOCK GENIUS

THE BLOCKS

Blocks can be made in many sizes but 6, 9, and 12-inch blocks are some of the most used by quilters. Their versatility makes them fit easily into 2 x 2, 3 x 3, 4 x 4, and 6 x 6 grids.

Incremental measurements for cutting block components are included on most quilting rulers making it easy to rotary cut pieces. No piece will have anything less than an 1/8-inch increment.

There are so many great resources for block designs, including books, internet resources, and vintage quilts. Most of the blocks, other than a few my friend Laurel and I designed, are over 100 years old. They have certainly stood the test of time.

I tried to correctly identify each block by name. But some had identical names but a different design or colorway. Flipping or turning a component can change a name and create a new block.

Take a look at Jacob's Ladder, page 123, and Wagon Tracks, page 130. The cutting instructions and components are the same. It's a perfect example of how orientation of a part and changing a color will change a block name.

GRIDS AND BLOCK STRUCTURE

Most quilt blocks are designed by using a base grid of squares. A grid is based on how a block is divided on two sides. The squares within the grid are all the same size. Below are the four grids used to make the blocks in this book.

2 x 2

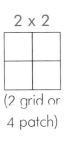 

(2 grid or
4 patch)

3 x 3

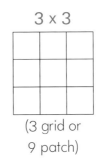 

(3 grid or
9 patch)

4 x 4

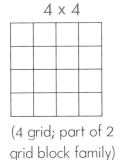 

(4 grid; part of 2
grid block family)

6 x 6

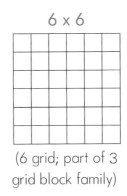 

(6 grid; part of 3
grid block family)

THE PARTS

Each square within the grid can be divided to create more pattern in the block. With each division, we can start to see other components besides squares; half- and quarter-square triangles, flying geese, or a square-in-a-square.

CUTTING CHARTS

In the block section, you'll see a photograph of each block, and cutting instructions with icons representing the pieces you will cut and subcut. Seam allowances are included in the measurements given for making 6, 9, and 12-inch finished blocks. All measurements are exact; there will be no trimming except for fabric "tails".

Colors are represented by letters with "A" being the lightest and "B, C, and D", representing medium to dark values. You can change your color choices based on these values and you will maintain the same look of the block.

An illustration of how the block is constructed is shown below the cutting chart. Instructions for piecing the components that make up the block are referenced by page number below the illustration.

Good to Know

After I cut all the pieces for a block, I laid them out beside my sewing machine, or on my ironing board, so I could sew the parts together in order. I liked being able to have a visual of the block instead of all the pieces sitting in piles in front of me. It saved time, too.

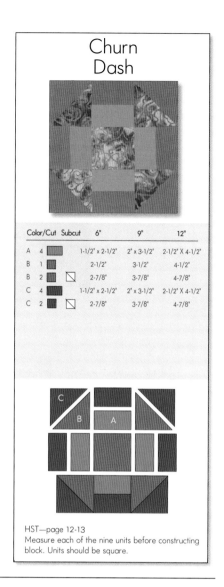

Churn Dash

Color/Cut	Subcut	6"	9"	12"
A 4		1-1/2" x 2-1/2"	2" x 3-1/2"	2-1/2" X 4-1/2"
B 1		2-1/2"	3-1/2"	4-1/2"
B 2	◻	2-7/8"	3-7/8"	4-7/8"
C 4		1-1/2" x 2-1/2"	2" x 3-1/2"	2-1/2" X 4-1/2"
C 2	◻	2-7/8"	3-7/8"	4-7/8"

HST—page 12-13
Measure each of the nine units before constructing block. Units should be square.

TO PIN OR NOT TO PIN?

For me, there is no cut and dried rule when it comes to using pins. I keep them handy but pick and choose when I use them. Since I was working with smaller pieces, I didn't pin every time I sewed. I tended to use pins more when I was sewing bias cut pieces and when I sewed segments together to construct a block. That way, my seams matched and my pieces stayed aligned. If you are a beginner, I suggest using pins more often than not. There is nothing I want more than for you to have a satisfying experience as you begin your block and quiltmaking journey!

SEWING SMALL PIECES

I discovered I was getting some wonkiness on some pieces because I couldn't hold on to them past my sewing machine foot. I found a stiletto came in handy when I got to the end of a seam. I could use the point to hold the pieces in line at the finish. But read on...leaders and enders can help, too.

Good to Know

If you need to undo your stitching, avoid pulling apart; you will resize pieces quicker than you realize by stretching the fabric. Using your ripping tool, lay your sewn piece flat, and cut every third or fourth stitch. Remove any thread and gently re-press before sewing.

CUTTING

I liked my 3-1/2 and 4-1/2 by 12-1/2-inch rulers, and my 6-1/2-inch square ruler, all with 1/8" increments. Because the fabric pieces were smaller, the rulers were easier to handle. Hold onto your rulers when you cut. The grippers on the back of mine didn't work as well with smaller pieces of fabric so applying a little more pressure was necessary when cutting.

QUARTER-INCH SEAMS

The cutting instructions include seam allowances, which is part of the "genius" feature. The math is done for you! It is important to sew accurate 1/4" seams. Being off just a thread or two adds up as you sew, either increasing or decreasing the size of your block.

I used my quarter-inch foot and extended the "line" with a piece of painter's tape taped to the throat of my machine. Use the tools that work best for you. Consistency is the key to accurate piecing. Switching from one machine to another, or switching out your tool of choice can make a huge difference in the way your blocks come together.

It's a good idea to sew a sample quarter-inch seam. Check the accuracy with whichever technique you choose and make adjustments accordingly.

LEADER AND ENDER SCRAPS

Sewing small pieces can be tricky when you begin your seam, especially if you are starting on the tip of a triangle. To keep the fabric from getting pulled down into the needle plate, use a small scrap of fabric, the "leader", followed by your pieces. When you come to the end of your seam, use another scrap, the "ender", stitch into it, and leave it under your machine foot. The ender has now become the leader for the next seam. Snip threads that connect your pieces to these scraps.

PRESSING

I don't necessarily follow the standard for pressing seams. Because I was only making one block at a time, I pressed my seams open so the block would lay flat.

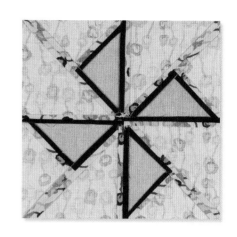

I understand the concept of pressing seams toward the darker fabric. I think this is important, especially if you are sewing light and dark fabrics together. If you choose to press the seams to the dark side, try this: Lay your sewn piece dark side up, open it, and press. The seams will automatically press to the dark side. (Finger pressing is a nice "assist" to get started with your iron.)

Take great care as you press the pieces of your block. I do believe in the "press, don't iron" rule. Lift your iron up and down instead of "ironing" from side to side. Steam or no steam? Again, it's a personal preference. I like a little bit but I also know I accidentally stretched my pieces more than I anticipated using steam. This is an instance where I knew better but I just had to do it my way. I paid the price with some time consuming do-overs!

Good to Know

When I finished a block, I did a last press with spray starch. It gives the block some additional stability. I sprayed the back of the block to make sure my seams stayed open, too.

COLOR

Making one block at a time gave me the opportunity to play around with color. It's a great way to use your scraps and stash. If you find a color combination you love and a block pattern you really like, then you have started the design process for an entire quilt.

I think color is a very personal thing. I like finding one color or fabric pattern and building from it. Use photos, paint chips, or a fabric collection as inspiration. And don't forget the color wheel. The science and theory represented in it is a surefire way to make your color choices theoretically correct and most appealing to the eye. Pick your favorite color on the wheel and try using the colors across and next to it. BUT, don't be afraid to experiment.

If you look at the blocks in this book, and you aren't crazy about my color choices, think about how you would change them to reflect your own preferences. This is the time to teach yourself how to look beyond what you see. Make a quick line sketch of the block if it helps to see the block without color. You can use grid paper if you want to be really exact. Use your colored pencils or markers to play around with your own colorways.

Getting Started

STEP-BY-STEP

You might be inclined to jump right to the block section, but I encourage you to run through the step-by-step instructions presented first. Because the blocks are made one at a time, I chose simple techniques that were sufficient to make each block, based on how I saw components within the block. I think practicing these techniques is a great way to build your piecing skills.

Since there are no measurements included in the step-by-step instructions, use the cutting chart for each block you are making and cut pieces that pertain to the size of your block. The step-by-step technique will move you forward through the piecing process. If you are a beginner, these instructions are basic enough to get you started. If you are an experienced quilter, you can apply your shortcut skills wherever you have an opportunity.

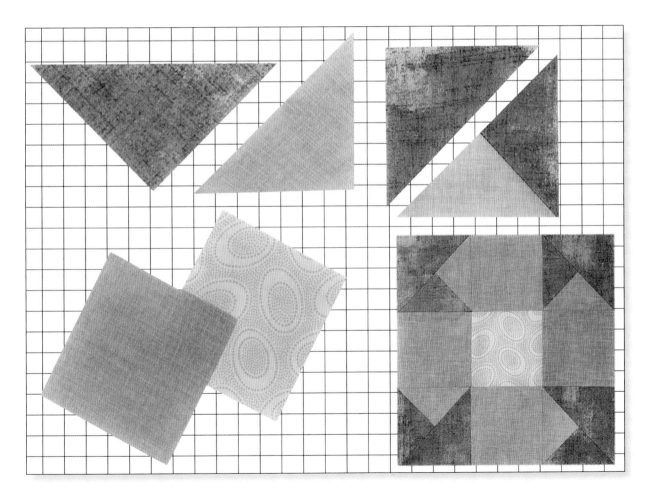

Half-Square Triangle Technique 1

Half-square triangles (HSTs) are used in a variety of block designs. The HST in this technique is made by cutting squares and then piecing two triangles together. To determine what size to cut fabric squares for HSTs, add 7/8-inch to the finished size of the square.

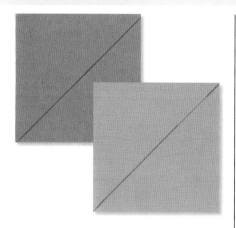

1 Using the measurements from the cutting chart, cut each square in half diagonally from corner to corner using a ruler and rotary cutter. (You can draw the diagonal line in pencil first if you are not confident holding your ruler in place.)

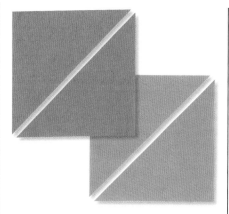

2 Each square will yield two triangles.

3 Layer a light and dark triangle, RST. Sew a 1/4" seam along the long edge of the triangles.

RST=right sides together

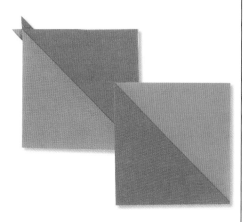

4 Press the seam open. Trim fabric "tails".

Zig Zag Block

Use the instructions for Half-Square Triangle Technique 1 to practice making the Zig Zag Triangle Block. There are a total of 16 HSTs made individually.

Color / Cut		Subcut	6"	9"	12"
A White 8	☐	◹	2-3/8"	3-1/8"	3-7/8"
B Floral 4	☐	◹	2-3/8"	3-1/8"	3-7/8"
C Blue 4	☐	◹	2-3/8"	3-1/8"	3-7/8"

Half Square Triangle Technique 2

With the second HST technique you will sew seams before cutting the squares into triangles. This method is particularly useful when making several HSTs. The only difference between techniques 1 and 2 is the way the HST is constructed.

1 Using the measurements from the cutting chart, draw a diagonal line from corner to corner on the wrong side of the lighter square. Layer a light and dark square, RST.

2 Sew a 1/4" seam on either side of the drawn line. (You can either draw a sewing line, shown here as a dashed line, or use your 1/4" machine foot.)

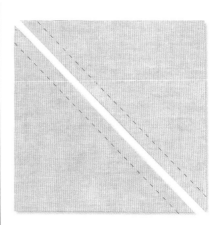

3 Cut on the drawn line.

4 Press the seams open. Trim fabric "tails".

Star of the West Block

Use the instructions for Half-Square Triangle Technique 2 to practice making the Star of the West Block. Since it is made from only 2 colors, this is the perfect technique to make HSTs two at a time.

Color / Cut	Subcut	6"	9"	12"
A White 8 ☐ ◪		2-3/8"	3-1/8"	3-7/8"
B Orange 8 ☐ ◪		2-3/8"	3-1/8"	3-7/8"

Quarter-Square Triangle Technique 1

The Quarter-Square Triangle (QST) block is also referred to as an Hourglass block. To determine the cutting size, add 1-1/4-inch to the finished size of the square for both QST techniques. Since you are sewing on the bias with this technique, handle gently to avoid stretching your pieces.

1 Using the measurements from the cutting chart, cut 2 contrasting squares. Draw a diagonal line, from corner to corner, in both directions. Cut each square on the drawn lines.

2 Each square will yield four triangles.

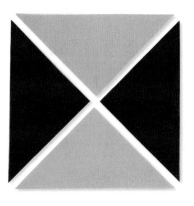

3 Lay out the block, alternating fabric as shown.

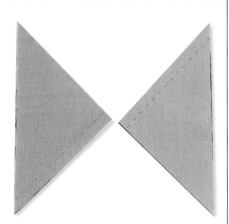

4 Layer a light and dark triangle, RST. Stitch with a 1/4" seam along a short edge of each pair of triangles. Press the seams toward the darker fabric.

RST=right sides together

5 Layer two pairs of triangles, RST with the light fabric on the dark, making sure seams are aligned. Sew a ¼" seam along the long edge of the pair.

6 Press the seam and trim the fabric "tails".

Quarter-Square Triangle Technique 2

This technique is particularly useful when making several QSTs. This method can be interchanged with QST technique 1, depending on how many you need to make. Fabric is less likely to stretch since you are sewing on an uncut square.

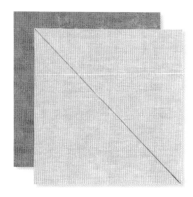

1 Using the measurements from the cutting chart, cut 2 squares of contrasting fabric. Draw a diagonal line from corner to corner on the wrong side of one block.

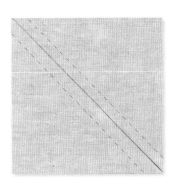

2 With RST, sew a 1/4" seam on either side of the drawn line. (You can either draw a sewing line, shown here as a dashed line, or use your 1/4" machine foot.)

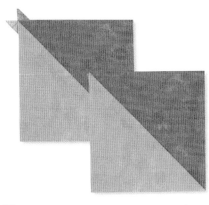

3 Cut on the diagonal line to make two HSTs. Press seams open and trim fabric "tails".

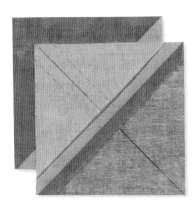

4 Place the HSTs together with the light fabric on top of the dark fabric, matching diagonal seams. Draw a diagonal line from corner to corner on the wrong side of one HST.

5 Sew a 1/4" seam on either side of the drawn line. Cut on the diagonal line and press seams open. Trim fabric "tails".

6 This method will make two QSTs.

Flying Geese From Triangles

Whether you are making one or a few flying geese, this technique is the most basic to create a goose. The large triangle is the "goose" body and the small triangles are the "sky". The body is cut from a quarter-square triangle. There may be left over pieces, depending on how many geese you make.

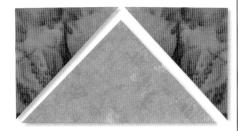

1 Use measurements from the cutting chart to create three triangles for a flying geese unit.

Note: The cutting chart will tell you to cut one square and subcut it diagonally twice from corner to corner. Depending on the block, you may have left over "body" triangles.

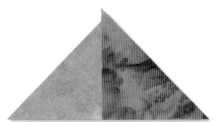

2 With RST, align the bottom and bias edge of a small "sky" triangle as shown. The corner of the "sky" should extend past the "goose".

RST=right sides together

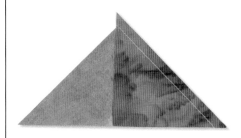

3 Pin if you prefer, and sew along the long side of the "sky" triangle with a 1/4" seam.

4 Press seam away from "goose".

5 In the same manner, add the second small "sky" triangle to the opposite side of the "goose". Stitch along the long side of the sky triangle with a 1/4" seam.

6 Press seam away from "goose" and trim fabric "tails".

Flying Geese From Squares

In the second technique, squares are added to each corner of a rectangle to create a goose. Pieces to be used for Flying Geese from Squares are marked with an asterisk (*) in the cutting chart.

1 Using the measurements from the cutting chart, cut a rectangle and 2 squares for a flying geese unit. Draw a diagonal line from corner to corner on the wrong side of each of the smaller squares.

2 With RST, layer one square on a corner of the rectangle. Sew on the drawn line. Trim 1/4" from seam. Press seam toward smaller triangle.

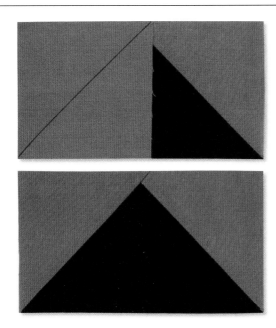

3 With RST, layer the second square on the opposite corner, as shown. Sew on the drawn line. Trim corner 1/4" from seam. Press seam toward smaller triangle.

Good to Know

When you need to draw a sewing line, remember that the sewing line IS the edge of your ruler and it's impossible to draw a line at that point. Be sure to use a sharp-tipped pen or pencil and tip your marking tool at an angle, as shown, to get as close to the edge of your ruler as possible.

Four-at-a-Time Flying Geese

This no-waste method will yield four Flying Geese. This is the technique to use when there are four identical flying geese within a block. Pieces to be used for Four-at-a-Time Flying Geese are marked with an asterisk (*) in the cutting chart.

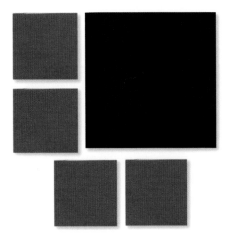

1 Using the measurements from the cutting chart, cut 1 large square for the "geese" and 4 small squares for the "sky" triangles.

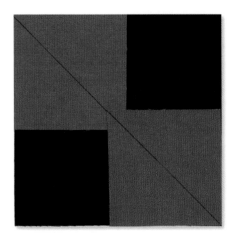

2 Draw a diagonal line from corner to corner on the wrong side of all four of the small squares. With RST, layer and pin two squares on opposite corners of the large square as shown.

RST=right sides together

3 Sew a 1/4" seam on either side of the drawn line. Cut on drawn line to make two units.

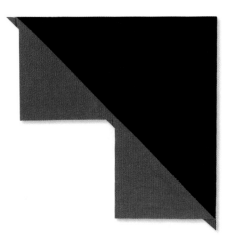

4 Press smaller triangles away from the larger triangle on each of the units in step 3.

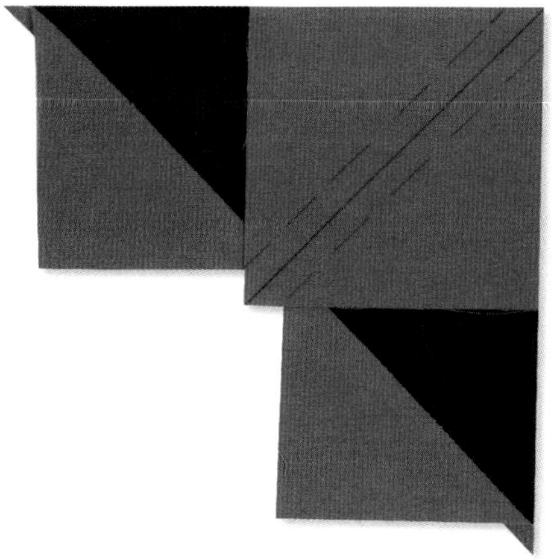

5 With RST, layer and pin one square on the corner of a unit from step 4.

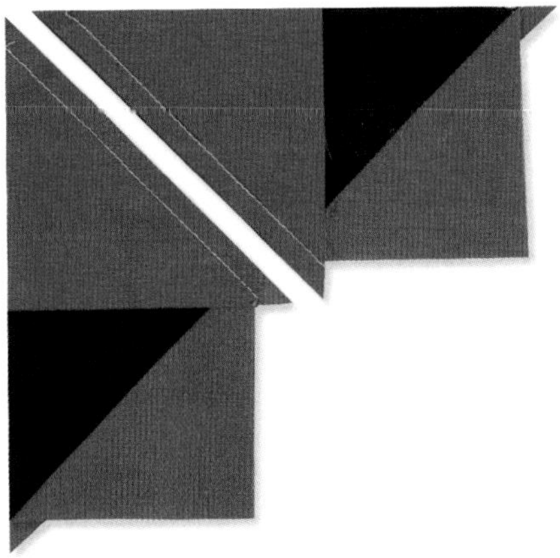

6 Sew a 1/4" seam on either side of the drawn line. Cut on the drawn line. Press seams away from larger triangle. Repeat with second large triangle unit.

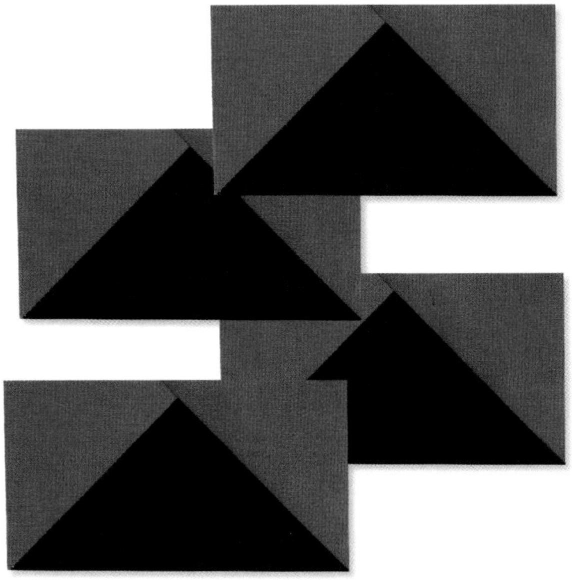

7 Press seams toward smaller triangles. Trim the fabric "tails".

Spinning Geese Block

Use the Four-at-a-Time Flying Geese technique to practice making the Spinning Geese Block.

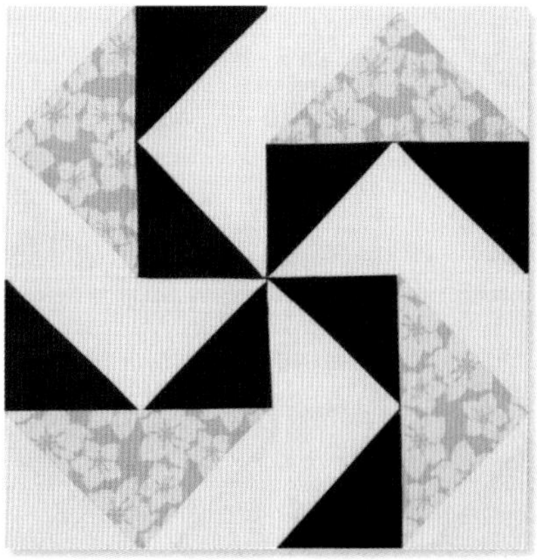

Color / Cut		Subcut	6"	9"	12"
A White	1 □	⧅	2-3/8"	3-1/8"	3-7/8"
A White	4 □	⧅	4-1/4"	5-3/4"	7-1/4"
B Floral	1 □	⧅	4-1/4"	5-3/4"	7-1/4"
C Navy	4 □	⧅	2-3/8"	3-1/8"	3-7/8"

Partial Seams

Partial seams are necessary when pieces "wrap" or "pinwheel" around a center square. There are only a couple of blocks in this book that use this technique but it's good to know how to sew these seams.

1 Using the measurements from the cutting chart, cut a square and four rectangles for the block.

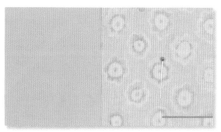

2 With RST, sew the first rectangle to the center, beginning from the middle of the center square and locking your starting stitches. Finger press seam.

RST=right sides together

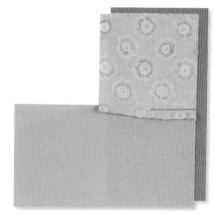

3 With RST, layer the partial seam unit from step 2 to the second rectangle, and sew 1/4" seam the length of the rectangle. Finger press the seam open.

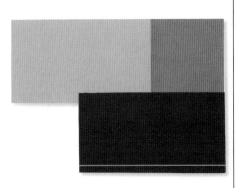

4 With RST, sew the third rectangle onto the unit. Finger press the seam open.

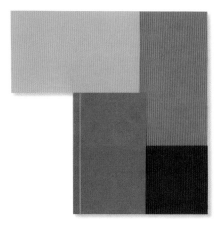

5 Repeat step 4 with the final rectangle.

6 Turn block right side up. It will have a partially unsewn rectangle, as shown, ready to be sewn to complete the block.

7 Flip the unsewn rectangle down and align with the top of the center block, RST. Sew 1/4" partial seam to complete the block.

8 Press seams.

Parallel Seams

The parallel component is used in several quilt blocks, including the Magnolia block, page 124, and Pudding and Pie, page 127. It can also be used alone to make a zigzag or chevron quilt. Pieces to be used for a Parallel component are marked with an asterisk (*) in the cutting chart.

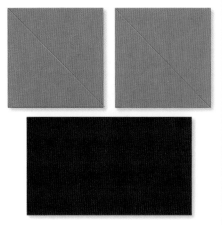

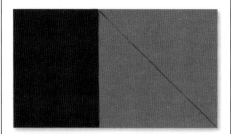

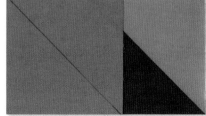

1 Using the measurements from the cutting chart, cut a rectangle and two squares. Draw a diagonal line from corner to corner on the wrong side of both small squares.

2 With RST, layer one square on top of the rectangle, as shown. Sew on drawn line. Trim 1/4" from sewn line.

RST=right sides together

3 Press seam open. Lay a small square on the opposite corner RST, with the drawn line parallel to first sewn line, as shown. Sew on drawn line. Trim 1/4" from seam.

4 Press seam open.

Note: See page 43 on how to use cutaway triangles.

Diamond Zig Zag Block

Use the Parallel Seams instructions to practice making the Diamond Zig Zag Block. Place 4 squares on rectangles with drawn lines facing left. Place the other 4 squares with sewn lines facing right. Parallel components should "mirror" one another to correctly make this block.

Color / Cut		6"	9"	12"
A Green 8		2" x 3-1/2"	2-3/4" x 5"	3-1/2" x 6-1/2"
B Floral 16		2"	2-3/4"	3-1/2"

Square-in-a-Square

This component is used in many block designs but can stand alone as a 2 x 2 grid block. The large center square can be fussy-cut for a different look.

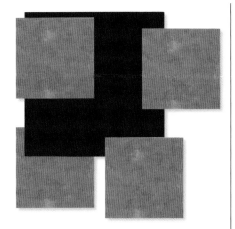

1 Using the measurements from the cutting chart, cut a large square and 4 small squares.

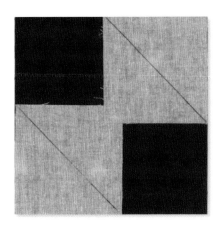

2 Draw a diagonal line from corner to corner on the wrong side of all 4 of the small squares. With RST, layer and pin two small squares on opposite corners as shown.

3 Sew on the drawn line. Trim corners 1/4" from seam.

Note: See page 43 on how to use cutaway triangles.

4 Press seams open.

5 Repeat with two additional squares on remaining corners as shown in step 3.

6 Trim 1/4" from seam and press seams open.

Note: This is a good block to check measurements after completed. Be sure it's square.

Adding Corners

These components are most often used to create more complex blocks, such as Flying Leaves, page 57 and Waypoint Star, page 110. Corners can be added to either squares or rectangles. Pieces to be used for these units are marked with an asterisk (*) in the cutting chart.

1 Using the measurements from the cutting chart, cut one rectangle and one square. Draw a diagonal line from corner to corner on the wrong side of the square.

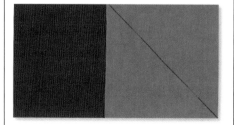

2 To make a right corner block, align a small square RST along the right side of the rectangle, as shown.

RST=right sides together

3 Sew on the drawn line. Trim 1/4" from seam. Press seam open.

4 For a left corner block, repeat step 2 aligning the smaller square RST along the left side of the rectangle.

Adding Triangles to a Square

The half-square triangles in the block below change the look dramatically by piecing a square and two triangles of contrasting color or pattern.

1 Cut a square and 2 triangles using the measurements in the cutting chart.

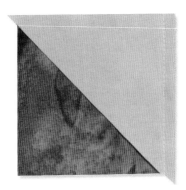

2 With RST, align the straight edge of the triangle to two sides of a square as shown. Sew on one short side using a 1/4" seam.

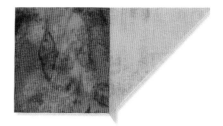

3 Press seam and trim the triangle "tail".

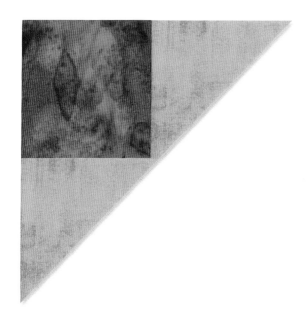

4 Align a second triangle to adjacent side of the square-triangle unit. Sew and press seam. Trim triangle "tail".

Triangles in a Row

A few blocks require sewing triangles together in a row. (See North Wind Block on page 66.) This technique is a must to guarantee the strip of triangles maintain their points when adding the other components of the block.

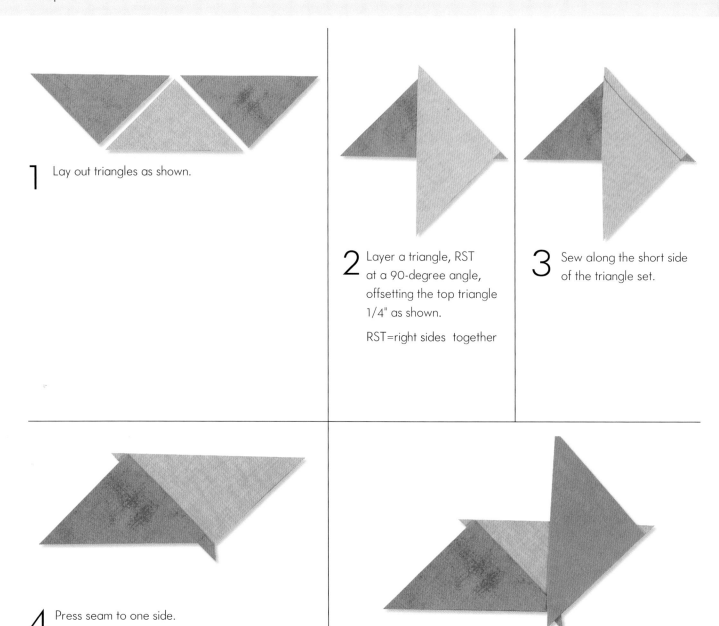

1 Lay out triangles as shown.

2 Layer a triangle, RST at a 90-degree angle, offsetting the top triangle 1/4" as shown.

RST=right sides together

3 Sew along the short side of the triangle set.

4 Press seam to one side.

5 Layer another triangle on top of set, offsetting a 1/4" as shown. Sew along the short side.

6 Press seam to one side. Trim the fabric "tails".

Good to Know

The more pieces in your block, the more pressing is necessary. I found that hanging my block over the edge of my ironing board made it easier to press seams without disturbing the ones I had already pressed.

The 2 x 2 Grid Blocks

A 2 x 2 grid block is a good starting point for beginners because the components are usually bigger. But the process is the same; accurate cutting, accurate seams, gentle pressing. The block can be as simple as a four-patch in two colors. Start dissecting and the block will reveal pinwheels, big flying geese, contrasting half-square triangles, and arrows.

Big
Dipper

Color/Cut		Subcut	6"	9"	12"
A	2 ⬜	⊠	4-1/4"	5-3/4"	7-1/4"
B	1 ⬛	⊠	4-1/4"	5-3/4"	7-1/4"
C	1 ▨	⊠	4-1/4"	5-3/4"	7-1/4"

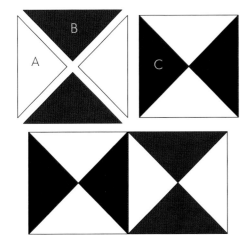

QST—pages 14-15

Broken
Dishes

Color/Cut		Subcut	6"	9"	12"
A	2 ⬜	◺	3-7/8"	5-3/8"	6-7/8"
B	2 ⬛	◺	3-7/8"	5-3/8"	6-7/8"

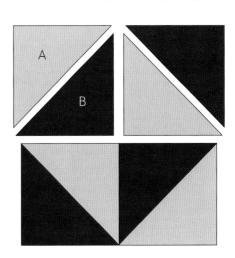

HST—pages 12-13

Buckeye Beauty

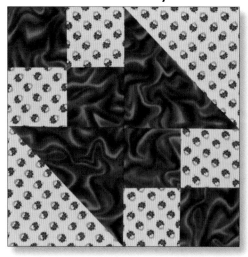

Color/Cut		Subcut	6"	9"	12"
A	4		2"	2-3/4"	3-1/2"
A	1	◹	3-7/8"	5-3/8"	6-7/8"
B	1	◹	3-7/8"	5-3/8"	6-7/8"
B	4		2"	2-3/4"	3-1/2"

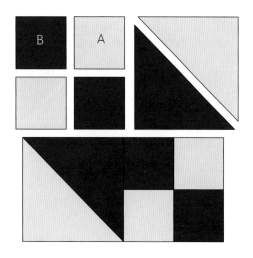

HST—pages 12-13

Carmen's Block

Color/Cut		Subcut	6"	9"	12"
A	2		3-1/2"	5"	6-1/2"
B	4		2"	2-3/4"	3-1/2"
C	4		2"	2-3/4"	3-1/2"

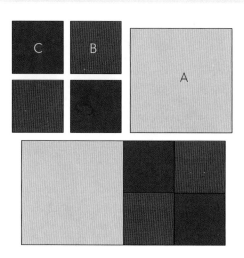

A good block to practice matching seams.

Caroline's Choice

Color/Cut		Subcut	6"	9"	12"
A	4	⬜ ◺	2-3/8"	3-1/8"	3-7/8"
B	2	⬜	3-1/2"	5"	6-1/2"
C	4	⬛ ◺	2-3/8"	3-1/8"	3-7/8"

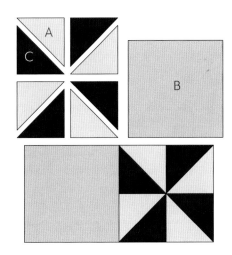

HST—pages 12-13
HSTs make a simple pinwheel.

Cracker Block

Color/Cut		Subcut	6"	9"	12"
A	1	⬜ ◺	3-7/8"	5-3/8"	6-7/8"
A	1	▭	2" x 4-3/4"	2-5/8" x 6-7/8"	3-3/8" x 9"
B	1	⬛ ◺	3-7/8"	5-3/8"	6-7/8"
B	2	▬	2" x 4-3/4"	2-5/8" x 6-7/8"	3-3/8" x 9"

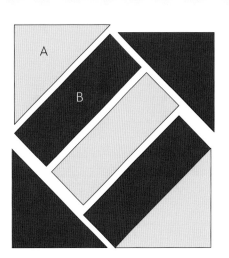

HST—pages 12-13

Crosses and Losses

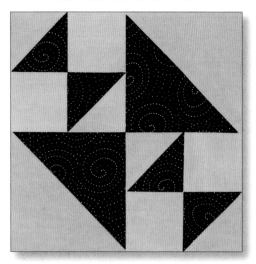

Color/Cut		Subcut	6"	9"	12"
A	1	◹	3-7/8"	5-3/8"	6-7/8"
A	4		2"	2-3/4"	3-1/2"
A	2	◹	2-3/8"	3-1/8"	3-7/8"
B	1	◹	3-7/8"	5-3/8"	6-7/8"
B	2	◹	2-3/8"	3-1/8"	3-7/8"

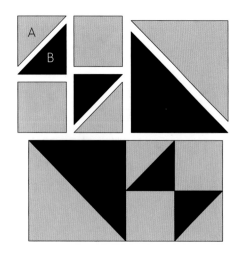

HST—pages 12-13

Double Pinwheel

Color/Cut		Subcut	6"	9"	12"
A	2	⊠	3-7/8"	5-3/8"	6-7/8"
B	1	⊠	4-1/4"	5-3/4"	7-1/4"
C	1	⊠	4-1/4"	5-3/4"	7-1/4"

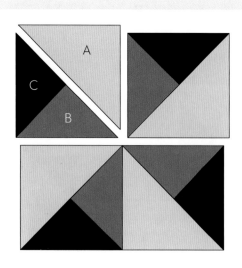

HST—pages 12-13
QST—page 14 (steps 1-4)

Double X Block

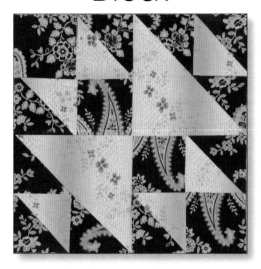

Color/Cut		Subcut	6"	9"	12"
A	1	◺	3-7/8"	5-3/8"	6-7/8"
A	3	◺	2-3/8"	3-1/8"	3-7/8"
B	4		2"	2-3/4"	3-1/2"
B	5	◺	2-3/8"	3-1/8"	3-7/8"

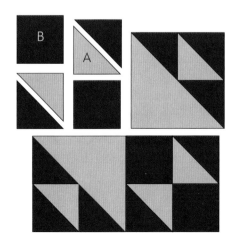

HST—pages 12-13
Adding Triangles to a Square—page 25

Flock of Geese

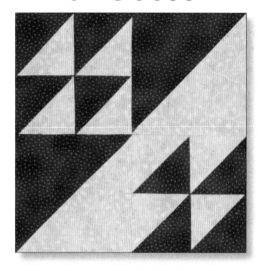

Color/Cut		Subcut	6"	9"	12"
A	1	◺	3-7/8"	5-3/8"	6-7/8"
A	4	◺	2-3/8"	3-1/8"	3-7/8"
B	1	◺	3-7/8"	5-3/8"	6-7/8"
B	4	◺	2-3/8"	3-1/8"	3-7/8"

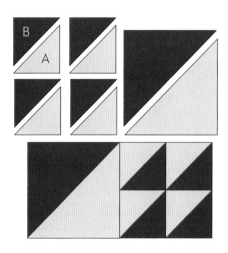

HST—pages 12-13
Check sizes of your HST's for accuracy before
putting this block together.

Flying Dutchman

Color/Cut		Subcut	6"	9"	12"
A	2	⊠	3-1/4"	4-1/4"	5-1/4
*A	8		1-1/2"	2"	2-1/2"
B	2	⊠	3-1/4"	4-1/4"	5-1/4"
*B	4		1-1/2" x 2-1/2"	2" x 3-1/2"	2-1/2" x 4-1/2"
B	4		1-1/2" x 3-1/2"	2" x 5"	2-1/2" x 6-1/2"

*Use 8 squares and 4 rectangles to make Flying Geese from Squares on page 17.

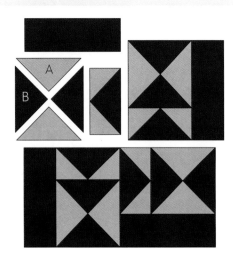

Flying Geese from Squares—page 17
QST—page 14

Forward and Back

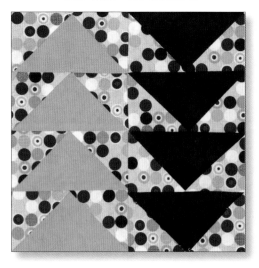

Color/Cut		Subcut	6"	9"	12"
A	4		2" x 3-1/2"	2-3/4" x 5"	3-1/2" x 6-1/2"
B	16		2"	2-3/4"	3-1/2"
C	4		2" x 3-1/2"	2-3/4" x 5"	3-1/2" x 6-1/2"

Note: Use the squares and rectangles to make Flying Geese from Squares on page 17.

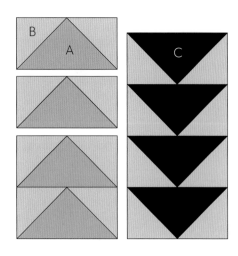

Flying Geese from Squares—page 17

Four Patch Variation

Color/Cut		Subcut	6"	9"	12"
A	2		2"	2-3/4"	3-1/2"
B	2		2"	2-3/4"	3-1/2"
B	2		2" x 3-1/2"	2-3/4" x 5"	3-1/2" x 6-1/2"
C	2		3-1/2"	5"	6-1/2"

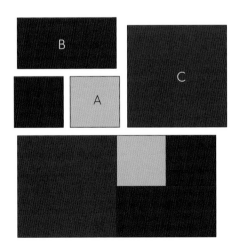

This is a simple block for a beginner. Make it in three sizes for practice.

Goday Design

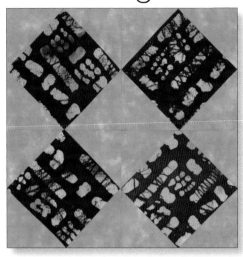

Color/Cut		Subcut	6"	9"	12"
A	16		2"	2-3/4"	3-1/2"
B	4		3-1/2"	5"	6-1/2"

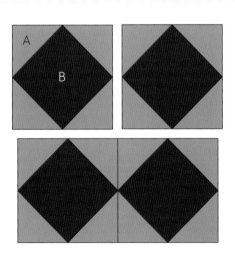

Square-in-a-Square—page 23
Check measurements of the square-in-a-square; it should be square! Trim if necessary.

Hidden Square

Color/Cut		Subcut	6"	9"	12"
A	1 ▨	◿	3-7/8"	5-3/8"	6-7/8"
B	1 ■		3-1/2"	5"	6-1/2"
B	1 ■	◿	6-7/8"	9-7/8"	12-7/8"

There will be a triangle left over from HST B subcut.

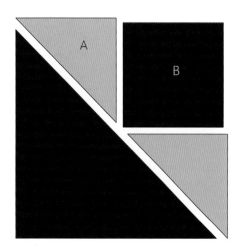

Adding Triangles to a Square—page 25

Homeward Bound

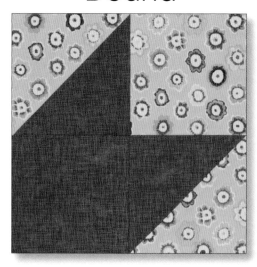

Color/Cut		Subcut	6"	9"	12"
A	1 ▨		3-1/2"	5"	6-1/2"
A	1 ▨	◿	3-7/8"	5-3/8"	6-7/8"
B	1 ■	◿	3-7/8"	5-3/8"	6-7/8"
B	1 ■		3-1/2"	5"	6-1/2"

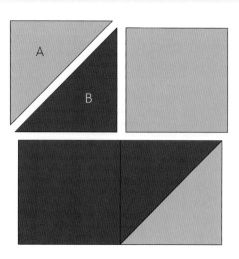

HST—pages 12-13

Linoleum Patch

Color/Cut		Subcut	6"	9"	12"
A	2		1-1/2" x 3-1/2"	2" x 5"	2-1/2" x 6-1/2"
B	2		3-1/2"	5"	6-1/2"
C	4		1-1/2" x 3-1/2"	2" x 5"	2-1/2" x 6-1/2"

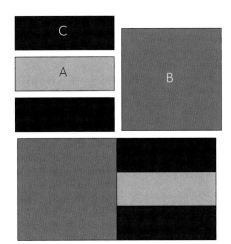

Check your quarter-inch seams when sewing A & C. Make sure the 3-strip unit is square.

Louisiana Pinwheel

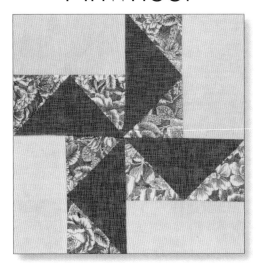

Color/Cut		Subcut	6"	9"	12"
A	4		2" x 3-1/2"	2-3/4" x 5"	3-1/2" x 6-1/2"
*B	8		2"	2-3/4"	3-1/2"
*C	4		2" x 3-1/2"	2-3/4" x 5"	3-1/2" x 6-1/2"

*Use B squares and C rectangles to make Flying Geese from Squares on page 17.

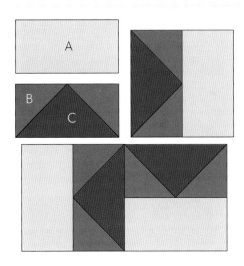

Flying Geese from Squares—page 17

Railroad Crossing

Color/Cut		Subcut	6"	9"	12"
A	1	◻ ◿	3-7/8"	5-3/8"	6-7/8"
A	4	◻	2"	2-3/4"	3-1/2"
B	4	◼	2"	2-3/4"	3-1/2"
C	1	◼ ◿	3-7/8"	5-3/8"	6-7/8"

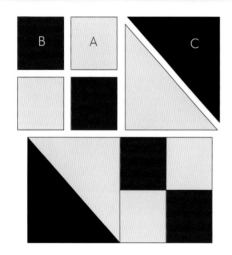

HST—pages 12-13

Right and Left

Color/Cut		Subcut	6"	9"	12"
A	1	◼	6-1/2"	9-1/2"	12-1/2"
A	2	◼ ◿	3-7/8"	5-3/8"	6-7/8"
B	2	◼ ◿	3-7/8"	5-3/8"	6-7/8"

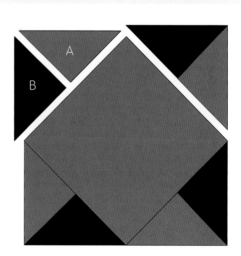

QST—pages 14 (steps 1-4)
Mark the center on each edge of the square.
It helps center the triangle sets.

Slanted
Diamonds

Color/Cut	Subcut		6"	9"	12"
A	4	⬜	3-1/2"	5"	6-1/2"
B	2	⬛	3-1/2" x 6-1/2"	5" x 9-1/2"	6-1/2" x 12-1/2"

Note: Use the squares and rectangles to make parallel seams on page 22.

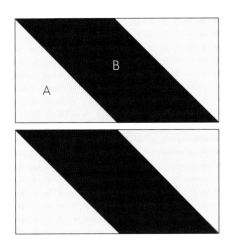

Parallel Seams—page 22

Southern
Belle

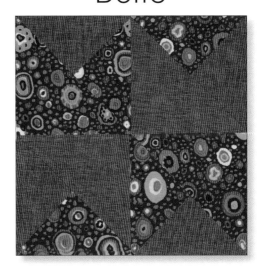

Color/Cut	Subcut		6"	9"	12"
A	1	▨ ⊠	3-7/8"	5-3/8"	6-7/8"
A	1	▨ ⊠	4-1/4"	5-3/4"	7-1/4"
B	1	⬛ ⊠	3-7/8"	5-3/8"	6-7/8"
B	1	⬛ ⊠	4-1/4"	5-3/4"	7-1/4"

The square component with three triangles is sometimes referred to as a "three patch quarter-square triangle".

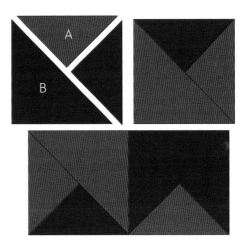

HST—pages 12-13
QST—page 14 (steps 1-4)

Spin City

Color/Cut		Subcut	6"	9"	12"
A	2	◹	3-7/8"	5-3/8"	6-7/8"
B	4		2"	2-3/4"	3-1/2"
C	4	◹	2-3/8"	3-1/8"	3-7/8"

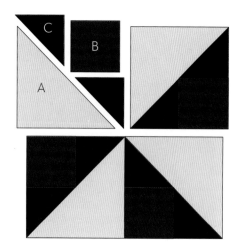

HST—pages 12-13
Adding Triangles to a Square—page 25

The Sickle

Color/Cut		Subcut	6"	9"	12"
A	4		2"	2-3/4"	3-1/2"
A	1	◹	3-7/8"	5-3/8"	6-7/8"
B	4		2"	2-3/4"	3-1/2"
C	1	◹	3-7/8"	5-3/8"	6-7/8"

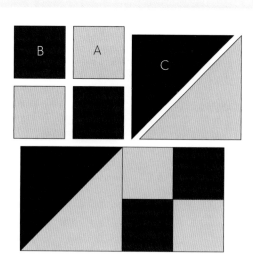

HST—pages 12-13

Turnstile Block

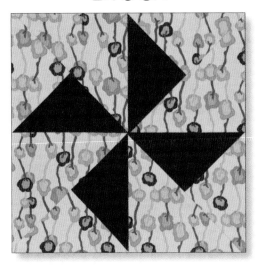

Color/Cut		Subcut	6"	9"	12"
A	2	⊠	3-7/8"	5-3/8"	6-7/8"
A	1	⊠	4-1/4"	5-3/4"	7-1/4"
B	1	⊠	4-1/4"	5-3/4"	7-1/4"

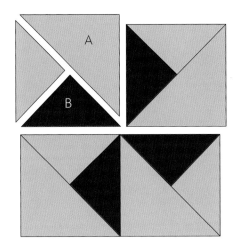

HST—pages 12-13
QST—page 14 (steps 1-4)

Two by Two

Color/Cut		Subcut	6"	9"	12"
A	4		2" x 3-1/2"	2-3/4" x 5"	3-1/2" x 6-1/2"
B	2		2" x 3-1/2"	2-3/4" x 5"	3-1/2" x 6-1/2"
C	2		2" x 3-1/2"	2-3/4" x 5"	3-1/2" x 6-1/2"

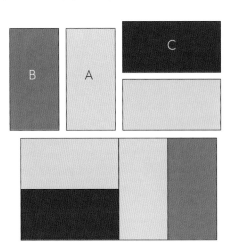

Another easy block using a rectangle shape.

Wild Geese Fancy Flight

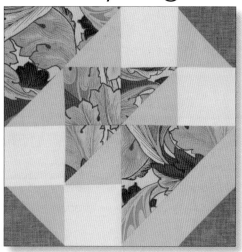

Color/Cut		Subcut	6"	9"	12"
A	1		2"	2-3/4"	3-1/2"
B	1	◺	3-7/8"	5-3/8"	6-7/8"
B	3	◺	2-3/8"	3-1/8"	3-7/8"
C	1	◺	2-3/8"	3-1/8"	3-7/8"
*C	1		2"	2-3/4"	3-1/2"
D	1	◺	2"	2-3/4"	3-1/2"
D	1		2"	2-3/4"	3-1/2"
D	1	◺	2-3/8"	3-1/8"	3-7/8"

There will be a left over B HST.
*For Adding Corners, page 24, use C square.

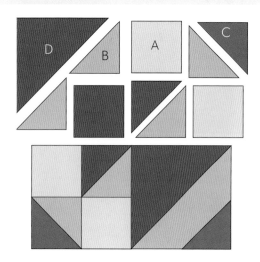

HST—pages 12-13; Adding Corners—page 24;
Adding Triangles to a Square—page 25

Wild Goose Chase

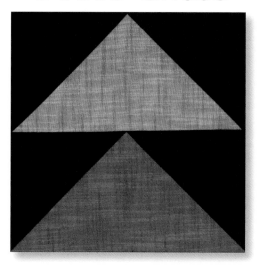

Color/Cut		Subcut	6"	9"	12"
*A	1		3-1/2" x 6-1/2"	5 x 9-1/2"	6-1/2" x 12-1/2"
*B	1		3-1/2" x 6-1/2"	5 x 9-1/2"	6-1/2" x 12-1/2"
*C	4		3-1/2"	5"	6-1/2"

*Use the squares and rectangles to make Flying Geese from Squares on page 17.

Note: This block can be made from 4-HSTs. But this technique alleviates a seam running through the "goose".

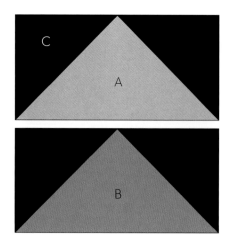

Flying Geese from Squares—page 17

Chain piecing is a time and thread-saver even in a single block. Anytime there are multiple pieces in a block, like these HSTs, give this technique a try.

1 Layer triangles, RST, as shown. Place a leader (page 9) under presser foot, sew off the edge, leaving thread, and follow with the first triangle set.

2 Without cutting the thread, continue adding triangle sets. You will have a long chain of pieces.

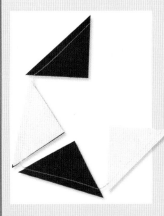

3 Snip threads that attach pieces. Press.

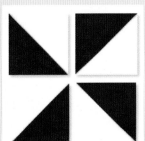

"Waste Triangles" are those corner pieces that are cut off when you use squares to make Flying Geese, parallel blocks, or other components. Here is a quick way to mark, sew and cut off corners and have the waste triangle ready to press and use in another project.

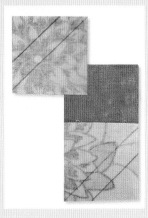

1 When you need to draw a sewing line corner to corner, draw an additional line 1/2-inch parallel to it. Sew on both lines.

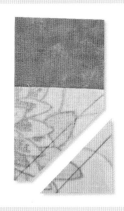

2 Cut between the lines creating two 1/4-inch seam allowances.

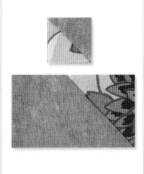

3 Press seams. Depending on the component you are making, you may have multiple HSTs. Each Flying Geese unit yields two leftover HSTs.

The 3 x 3 Grid Blocks

Detail starts to surface in 3 x 3 grid blocks because there are nine identical squares that can be divided and sub-divided. An hour glass, flying geese, and spinning pinwheels appear as you increase the sub-division and complexity of the block. 3 x 3 grid blocks sit very well next to 6 x 6 grid blocks of the same size in a quilt setting. The seams align to give an even appearance.

A Dandy Quilt Block

Color/Cut		Subcut	6"	9"	12"
*A	8		1-1/2"	2"	2-1/2"
B	2	◺	2-7/8"	3-7/8"	4-7/8"
C	1		2-1/2"	3-1/2"	4-1/2"
C	2	◺	2-7/8"	3-7/8"	4-7/8"
*D	4		2-1/2"	3-1/2"	4-1/2"

*For Adding Corners, page 24, use A squares and D squares.

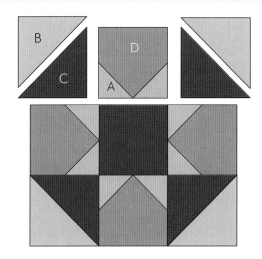

HST—pages 12-13
Adding Corners—page 24

Air Castle

Color/Cut		Subcut	6"	9"	12"
A	2	◺	2-7/8"	3-7/8"	4-7/8"
A	1	⊠	3-1/4"	4-1/4"	5-1/4"
B	1	⊠	3-1/4"	4-1/4"	5-1/4"
B	2	◺	2-7/8"	3-7/8"	4-7/8"
C	2	◺	2-7/8"	3-7/8"	4-7/8"
C	4		1-1/2"	2"	2-1/2"
D	1		2-1/2"	3-1/2"	4-1/2"

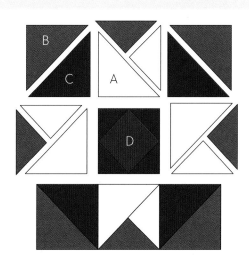

HST—pages 12-13; QST—page 14 (steps 1-4)
Square-in-a-Square—page 23

Album Star

Color/Cut		Subcut	6"	9"	12"
A	4		2"	2-3/4"	3-1/2"
A	1	⊠	4-1/4"	5-3/4"	7-1/4"
A	1		1-1/2" x 3-1/2"	2" x 5"	2-1/2 x 6-1/2"
B	4	◻	2-3/8"	3-1/8"	3-7/8"
B	2		1-1/2'" x 3-1/2"	2" x 5"	2-1/2 x 6-1/2"

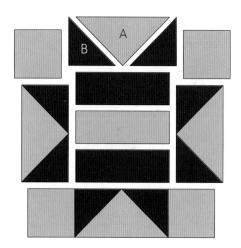

Flying Geese from Triangles—page 16

Antique Tiles

Color/Cut		Subcut	6"	9"	12"
A	4		1-1/2" x 2-1/2"	2" x 3-1/2"	2-1/2" x 4-1/2"
B	4		1-1/2" x 2-1/2"	2" x 3-1/2"	2-1/2" x 4-1/2"
B	4		1-1/2"	2"	2-1/2"
C	1		2-1/2"	3-1/2"	4-1/2"
C	4		1-1/2" x 2-1/2"	2" x 3-1/2"	2-1/2" x 4-1/2"
C	4		1-1/2"	2"	2-1/2"

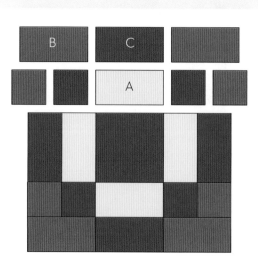

Lots of seams to match in this block! It will help to use pins when piecing this block.

Art Square

Color/Cut		Subcut	6"	9"	12"
A	4		2"	2-3/4"	3-1/2"
B	1		3-1/2"	5"	6-1/2"
*B	4		2" x 3-1/2"	2-3/4" x 4-3/4"	3-1/2" x 6-1/2"
*C	8		2"	2-3/4"	3-1/2"

*Use C squares and B rectangles to make Flying Geese from Squares, page 17.

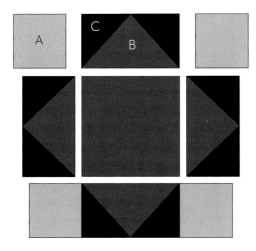

Flying Geese from Squares—page 17

Aunt Malvernia

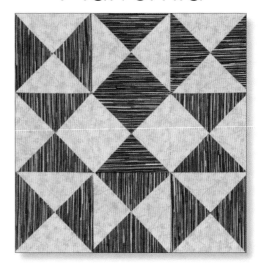

Color/Cut		Subcut	6"	9"	12"
A	5	⊠	3-1/4"	4-1/4"	5-1/4"
B	5	⊠	3-1/4"	4-1/4"	5-1/4"

There will be triangles left over from A and B QST subcuts.

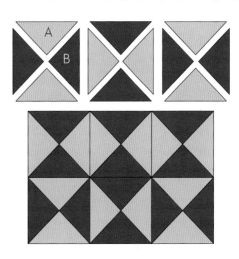

QST—pages 14-15
Pay attention to orientation of QSTs.

Balkan Variation

Color/Cut		Subcut	6"	9"	12"
A	1 ⬜		3-1/2"	5"	6-1/2"
A	4 ⬜	◩	2-3/8"	3-1/8"	3-7/8"
*B	4 ◼		2"	2-3/4"	3-1/2"
B	2 ◼	◩	2-3/8"	3-1/8"	3-7/8"
C	4 ◼		2"	2-3/4"	3-1/2"
*C	4 ▬		2" x 3-1/2"	2-3/4" x 5"	3-1/2" x 6-1/2"

*Use A and B squares, and C rectangles to make Flying Geese from Squares, page 17.

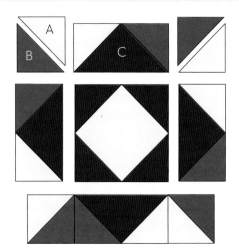

HST—pages 12-13; Square-in-a-Square—page 23
Flying Geese from Squares—page 17
Each goose has "light and dark" sky colors.

Bell's Favorite

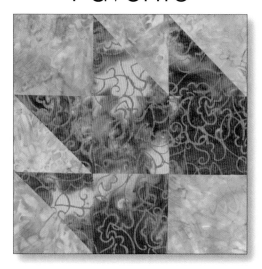

Color/Cut		Subcut	6"	9"	12"
A	2 ◼		2-1/2"	3-1/2"	4-1/2"
A	2 ◼	◪	2-7/8"	3-7/8"	4-7/8"
B	2 ◼	◪	2-7/8"	3-7/8"	4-7/8"
B	3 ◼		2-1/2"	3-1/2"	4-1/2"

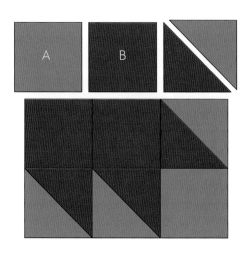

HST—pages 12-13

Bear Tracks

Color/Cut		Subcut	6"	9"	12"
A	2		2" x 3-1/2"	2-3/4" x 5"	3-1/2" x 6-1/2"
A	8		2"	2-3/4"	3-1/2"
B	4		2"	2-3/4"	3-1/2"
B	2		3-1/2"	5"	6-1/2"

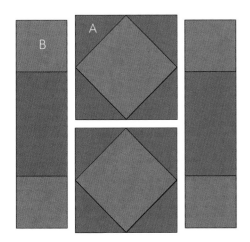

Square-in-a-Square—page 23

Big O Block

Color/Cut		Subcut	6"	9"	12"
A	1		2-1/2"	3-1/2"	4-1/2"
A	2	◹	2-7/8"	3-7/8"	4-7/8"
B	2	◹	2-7/8"	3-7/8"	4-7/8"
B	4		2-1/2"	3-1/2"	4-1/2"

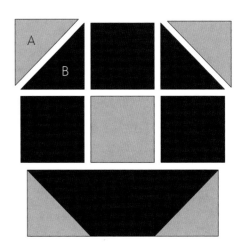

HST—pages 12-13

Big T Block

Color/Cut		Subcut	6"	9"	12"
A	2	⊠ (◻/)	2-7-8"	3-7/8"	4-7/8"
*A	1	⊠	3-1/4"	4-1/4"	5-1/4"
B	4	▭	1-1/2" x 2-1/2"	2" x 3-1/2"	2-1/2" x 4-1/2"
*C	4	◻/	1-7/8"	2-3/8"	2-7/8"
D	1		2-1/2"	3-1/2"	4-1/2"
D	2	◻/	2-7/8"	3-7/8"	4-7/8"

*Use the QST pieces for "body" of flying geese and HSTs for "sky" to make Flying Geese from Triangles, page 16.

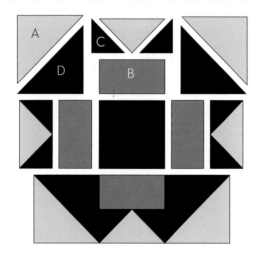

HST—pages 12-13
Flying Geese from Triangles—page 16

Birds In The Air

Color/Cut		Subcut	6"	9"	12"
A	1	◻/	6-7/8"	9-7/8"	12-7/8"
A	2	◻/	2-7-8"	3-7/8"	4-7/8"
B	3	◻/	2-7-8"	3-7/8"	4-7/8"

There will be triangles left over from both A HST subcuts.

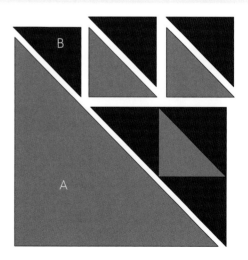

HST—pages 12-13; Adding Triangles to a Square—page 25. Make the large pieced triangle then sew to "A" triangle on the diagonal.

Birds In The Air Variation

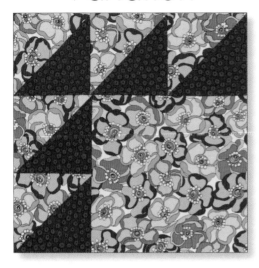

Color/Cut		Subcut	6"	9"	12"
A	1		4-1/2"	6-1/2"	8-1/2"
A	3	◻	2-7/8"	3-7/8"	4-7/8"
B	3	◻	2-7/8"	3-7/8"	4-7/8"

There will be triangles left over from A & B HST subcuts.

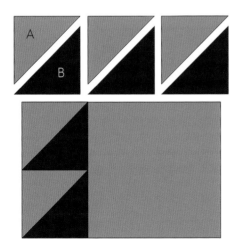

HST—pages 12-13

Blades Block

Color/Cut		Subcut	6"	9"	12"
A	2	◻	2-7/8"	3-7/8"	4-7/8"
B	1		2-1/2"	3-1/2"	4-1/2"
C	4		1-1/2"	2'	2-1/2"
D	2	◻	2-7/8"	3-7/8"	4-7/8"
D	4		1-1/2"	2'	2-1/2"
D	4		1-1/2" x 2-1/2"	2" x 3-1/2"	2-1/2" x 4-1/2"

Block designed by Sue Voegtlin

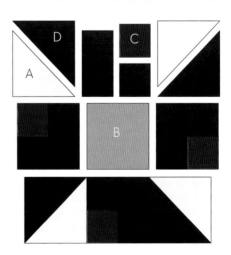

HST—pages 12-13
Pay attention to the orientation of the 4 corner HSTs.

Blocks In A Row

Color/Cut		Subcut	6"	9"	12"
A	1		2-1/2"	3-1/2"	4-1/2"
B	2		2-1/2"	3-1/2"	4-1/2"
B	2		2-1/2" x 6-1/2"	3-1/2" x 9-1/2"	4-1/2" x 12-1/2"

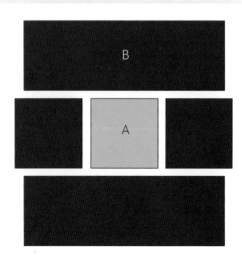

You can "fussy cut" the A block as shown, or use a contrasting solid.

Bright Hopes

Color/Cut		Subcut	6"	9"	12"
A	1		2-1/2"	3-1/2"	4-1/2"
B	1		2-1/2 x 4-1/2"	3-1/2" x 6-1/2"	4-1/2" x 8-1/2"
C	1		2-1/2 x 4-1/2"	3-1/2" x 6-1/2"	4-1/2" x 8-1/2"
D	1		2-1/2 x 4-1/2"	3-1/2" x 6-1/2"	4-1/2" x 8-1/2"
E	1		2-1/2 x 4-1/2"	3-1/2" x 6-1/2"	4-1/2" x 8-1/2"

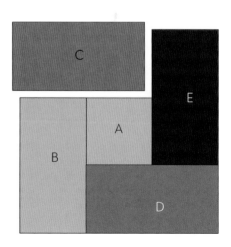

Partial Seams—page 20

Calico
Puzzle

Color/Cut		Subcut	6"	9"	12"
A	2 ▢	◺	2-7/8"	3-7/8"	4-7/8"
B	2 ▨	◺	2-7/8"	3-7/8"	4-7/8"
B	1 ▨		2-1/2"	3-1/2"	4-1/2"
C	4 ■		2-1/2"	3-1/2"	4-1/2"

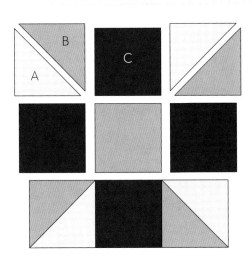

HST—pages 12-13
Pay attention to the orientation of the corner HSTs.

Card
Trick

Color/Cut		Subcut	6"	9"	12"
A	2 ▨	◺	2-7/8"	3-7/8"	4-7/8"
A	1 ▨	⊠	3-1/4"	4-1/4"	5-1/4"
B	1 ■	◺	2-7/8"	3-7/8"	4-7/8"
B	1 ■	⊠	3-1/4"	4-1/4"	5-1/4"
C	1 ■	◺	2-7/8"	3-7/8"	4-7/8"
C	1 ■	⊠	3-1/4"	4-1/4"	5-1/4"
D	1 ■	◺	2-7/8"	3-7/8"	4-7/8"
D	1 ■	⊠	3-1/4"	4-1/4"	5-1/4"
E	1 ■	◺	2-7/8"	3-7/8"	4-7/8"
E	1 ■	⊠	3-1/4"	4-1/4"	5-1/4"

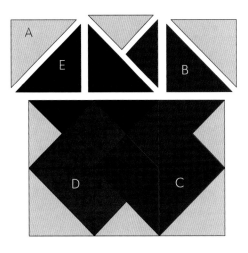

HST—pages 12-13; QST—page 14 (steps 1-4)
You will have triangles left over from B, C,
D, & E QST subcuts.

Celestial Block

Color/Cut		Subcut	6"	9"	12"
A	4		2"	2-3/4"	3-1/2"
B	1	◻	2-3/8"	3-1/8"	3-7/8"
C	1	◻	3-7/8"	5-3/8"	6-7/8"
D	1	◻	2-3/8"	3-1/8"	3-7/8"
E	1	◻	3-7/8"	5-3/8"	6-7/8"
F	2		2"	2-3/4"	3-1/2"
F	2	◻	2-3/8"	3-1/8"	3-7/8"
F	2		2" x 3-1/2"	2-3/4" x 5"	3-1/2" x 6-1/2"

There will be triangles left over from C & E HST subcuts.

Block designed by Laurel Albright

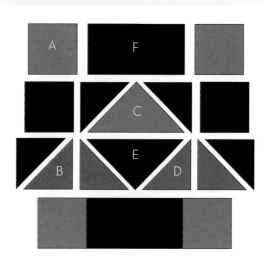

HST—pages 12-13
Flying Geese from Triangles—page 16

Churn Dash

Color/Cut		Subcut	6"	9"	12"
A	4		1-1/2" x 2-1/2"	2" x 3-1/2"	2-1/2" X 4-1/2"
B	1		2-1/2"	3-1/2"	4-1/2"
B	2	◻	2-7/8"	3-7/8"	4-7/8"
C	4		1-1/2" x 2-1/2"	2" x 3-1/2"	2-1/2" X 4-1/2"
C	2	◻	2-7/8"	3-7/8"	4-7/8"

HST—pages 12-13
Measure each of the nine units before constructing block. Units should be square.

Combination Star

Color/Cut		Subcut	6"	9"	12"
A	16		1-1/2"	2"	2-1/2"
A	2	⊠	3-1/4"	4-1/4"	5-1/4"
B	5		2-1/2"	3-1/2"	4-1/2"
C	2	⊠	3-1/4"	4-1/4"	5-1/4"

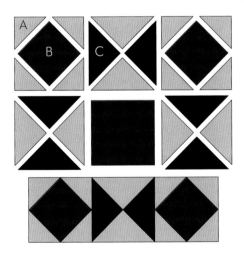

QST—page 15
Square-in-a-Square—page 23

Double Monkey Wrench

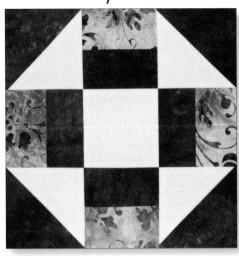

Color/Cut		Subcut	6"	9"	12"
A	1		2-1/2"	3-1/2"	4-1/2"
A	2	◹	2-7/8"	3-7/8"	4-7/8"
B	4		1-1/2" x 2-1/2"	2" x 3-1/2"	2-1/2" x 4-1/2"
C	4		1-1/2" x 2-1/2"	2" x 3-1/2"	2-1/2" x 4-1/2"
C	2	◹	2-7/8"	3-7/8"	4-7/8"

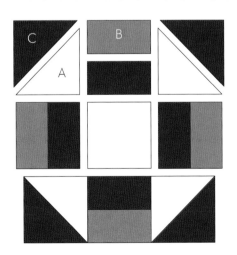

HST—pages 12-13
Experiment with this block by switching lights and darks.

Double Necktie

Color/Cut		Subcut	6"	9"	12"
A	4		2-1/2"	3-1/2"	4-1/2"
*A	4		1-1/2"	2"	2-1/2"
*B	5		2-1/2"	3-1/2"	4-1/2"

*For Adding Corners, page 24, use 4-A squares and 3-B squares.

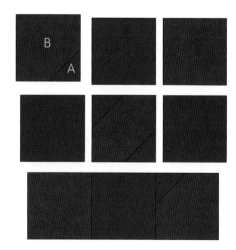

Adding Corners—page 24

Double X Block

Color/Cut		Subcut	6"	9"	12"
A	2	◺	2-7/8"	3-7/8"	4-7/8"
B	1		2-1/2"	3-1/2"	4-1/2"
C	1	◺	2-7/8"	3-7/8"	4-7/8"
D	2		2-1/2"	3-1/2"	4-1/2"
D	3	◺	2-7/8"	3-7/8"	4-7/8"

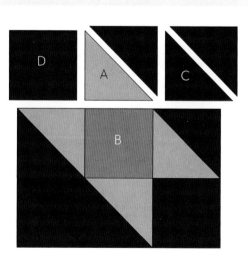

HST—pages 12-13
This is a good block to lay out all of the pieces correctly, then sew in rows.

Eccentric Star

Color/Cut		Subcut	6"	9"	12"
A	4 ⬜	◺	2-7/8"	3-7/8"	4-7/8"
B	2 ⬜	◺	2-7/8"	3-7/8"	4-7/8"
B	1 ⬜		2-1/2"	3-1/2"	4-1/2"
C	2 ⬛	◺	2-7/8"	3-7/8"	4-7/8"

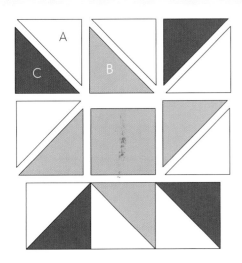

HST—pages 12-13
Pay attention to the orientation of HSTs in this block.

Flying Leaves

Color/Cut		Subcut	6"	9"	12"
*A	9 ⬜		2-1/2"	3-1/2"	4-1/2"
*B	10 ⬛		1-1/2"	2"	2-1/2"

For Adding Squares, page 24, use 6-A squares and 10-B squares.

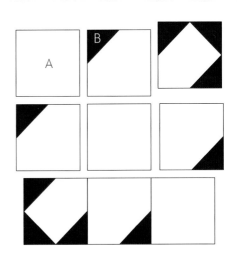

Adding Corners—page 24

Four Square

Color/Cut	Subcut	6"	9"	12"
A 8 ⬜		1-1/2"	2"	2-1/2"
B 8 ⬛		1-1/2"	2"	2-1/2"
B 1 ⬛		2-1/2"	3-1/2"	4-1/2"
C 4 ⬛		2-1/2"	3-1/2"	4-1/2"

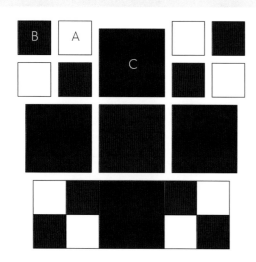

Make sure pieced squares are square in this 3 x 3 grid.

Four Square Variation

Color/Cut	Subcut	6"	9"	12"
A 8 ⬜		1-1/2"	2"	2-1/2"
A 4 ⬜		2-1/2"	3-1/2"	4-1/2"
B 8 ⬛		1-1/2"	2"	2-1/2"
B 1 ⬛		2-1/2"	3-1/2"	4-1/2"

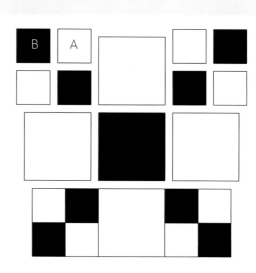

This variation of the Four Square Block is nothing more than a color change.

Gallery Star

Color/Cut		Subcut	6"	9"	12"
A	5		2-1/2"	3-1/2"	4-1/2"
A	1	⊠	3-1/4"	4-1/4"	5-1/4"
B	1	⊠	3-1/4"	4-1/4"	5-1/4"
C	1	⊠	3-1/4"	4-1/4"	5-1/4"
D	1	⊠	3-1/4"	4-1/4"	5-1/4"

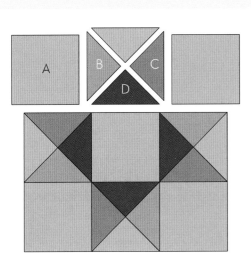

QST—page 14
Pay attention to color orientation in QSTs.

Green River

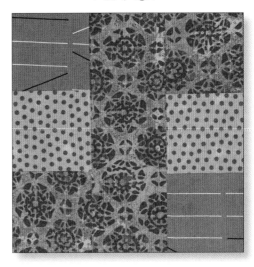

Color/Cut		Subcut	6"	9"	12"
A	2		2-1/2"	3-1/2"	4-1/2"
B	2		2-1/2"	3-1/2"	4-1/2"
C	2		2-1/2"	3-1/2"	4-1/2"
C	1		2-1/2" x 6-1/2"	3-1/2" x 9-1/2"	4-1/2" x 12-1/2"

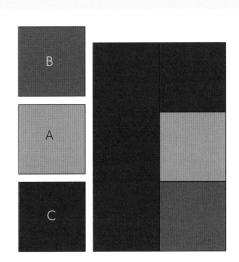

Hands of Friendship

Color/Cut		Subcut	6"	9"	12"
A	4 ☐		2-1/2"	3-1/2"	4-1/2"
A	1 ☐	⊠	3-1/4"	4-1/4"	5-1/4"
B	1 ☐	⊠	3-1/4"	4-1/4"	5-1/4"
B	1 ☐	⊠	4"	5-1/2"	7"
C	1 ☐	⊠	3-1/4"	4-1/4"	5-1/4"
C	1 ☐	⊠	4"	5-1/2"	7"

There will be one extra QST.

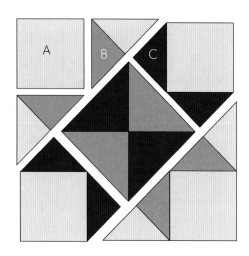

QST—page 14
Adding Triangles to a Square—page 25

Hovering Hawks

Color/Cut		Subcut	6"	9"	12"
A	2 ☐	◺	2-7/8"	3-7/8"	4-7/8"
B	6 ☐	◺	1-7/8"	2-3/8"	2-7/8"
C	2 ☐	◺	1-7/8"	2-3/8"	2-7/8"
C	5 ☐		2-1/2"	3-1/2"	4-1/2"

Make the B/C small half-square triangles first. Then sew the other B triangles to either side of the HST. Add an A triangle to complete unit.

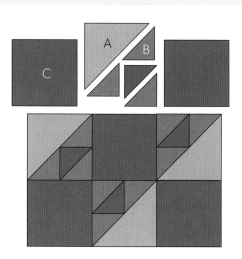

HST—pages 12-13
Adding Triangles to a Square—page 25

Indian Puzzle

Color/Cut		Subcut	6"	9"	12"
A	1		2-1/2"	3-1/2"	4-1/2"
A	4	◩	2-7/8"	3-7/8"	4-7/8"
B	4	◩	2-7/8"	3-7/8"	4-7/8"
B	4		1-1/2"	2'	2-1/2"

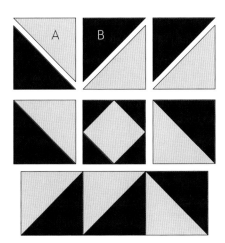

HST—pages 12-13
Square-in-a-Square—page 23

King's Crown

Color/Cut		Subcut	6"	9"	12"
A	1		3-1/2"	5"	6-1/2"
A	4		2" x 3-1/2"	2-3/4" x 5"	3-1/2" x 6-1/2"
B	8		2"	2-3/4"	3-1/2"

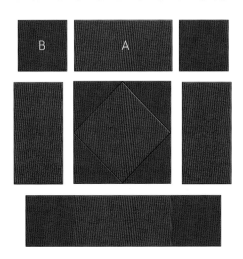

Square-in-a-Square—page 23

Ladies' Aid Album Quilt Block

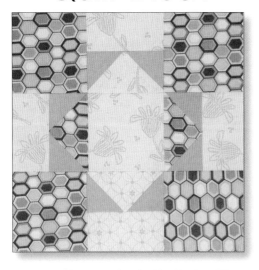

Color/Cut		Subcut	6"	9"	12"
A	1		2-1/2"	3-1/2"	4-1/2"
*A	6		1-1/2" x 2-1/2"	2" x 3-1/2"	2-1/2" x 4-1/2"
*B	8		1-1/2"	2"	2-1/2"
C	4		2-1/2"	3-1/2"	4-1/2"
*C	2		1-1/2" x 2-1/2"	2" x 3-1/2"	2-1/2" x 4-1/2"

*Use 2, A & C rectangles and B squares to make Flying Geese from Squares on page 17.

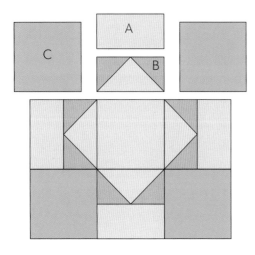

Flying Geese from Squares—page 17

Massachusetts Block

Color/Cut		Subcut	6"	9"	12"
A	1		2-1/2"	3-1/2"	4-1/2"
A	2	◻	2-7/8"	3-7/8"	4-7/8"
A	2	⊠	3-1/4"	4-1/4"	5-1/4"
B	1		2-1/2"	3-1/2"	4-1/2"
B	2	◻	2-7/8"	3-7/8"	4-7/8"
B	2	⊠	3-1/4"	4-1/4"	5-1/4"

There will be triangles left over from A & B HST subcuts.

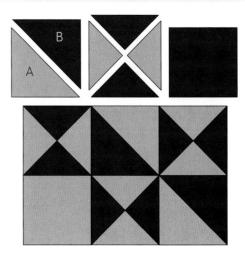

HST—pages 12-13
QST—page 14

Mississippi Block

Color/Cut		Subcut	6"	9"	12"
A	1		2-1/2"	3-1/2"	4-1/2"
*A	8		1-1/2"	2"	2-1/2"
*B	8		2-1/2"	3-1/2"	4-1/2"

For Adding Corners, page 24, use 8-A squares and 4-B squares.

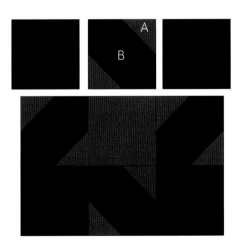

Adding Corners—page 24

Monkey Wrench

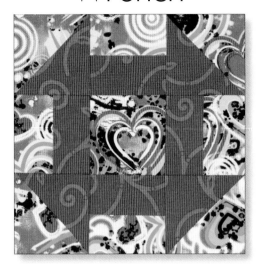

Color/Cut		Subcut	6"	9"	12"
A	1		2-1/2"	3-1/2"	4-1/2"
A	2	◻	2-7/8"	3-7/8"	4-7/8"
A	4		1-1/2" x 2-1/2"	2" x 3-1/2"	2-1/2" x 4-1/2"
B	2	◻	2-7/8"	3-7/8"	4-7/8"
B	4		1-1/2" x 2-1/2"	2" x 3-1/2"	2-1/2" x 4-1/2"

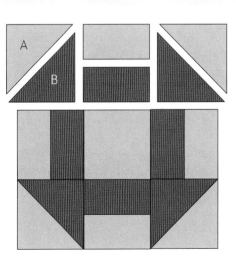

HST—pages 12-13

Mosaic 14 Block

Color/Cut		Subcut	6"	9"	12"
*A	16		2"	2-3/4"	3-1/2"
B	2		3-1/2"	5"	6-1/2"
*B	3		2" x 3-1/2"	2-3/4" x 5"	3-1/2" x 6-1/2"

*Use 6-A squares and 3-B rectangles to make Flying Geese from Squares on page 17.

Flying Geese from Squares—page 17
Square-in-a-Square—page 23

Mystery Garden

Color/Cut		Subcut	6"	9"	12"
A	1	⊠	3-1/4"	4-1/4"	5-1/4"
B	1		2-1/2"	3-1/2"	4-1/2"
B	2	⊠	3-1/4"	4-1/4"	5-1/4"
C	2	⊠	3-1/4"	4-1/4"	5-1/4"
C	2	⊡	2-7/8"	3-7/8"	4-7/8"
D	1	⊠	3-1/4"	4-1/4"	5-1/4"

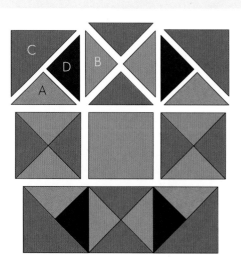

HST—pages 12-13
QST—page 15

Night Vision

Color/Cut		Subcut	6"	9"	12"
A	2	◻	2-7/8"	3-7/8"	4-7/8"
B	1		2-1/2"	3-1/2"	4-1/2"
B	2	◻	2-7/8"	3-7/8"	4-7/8"
C	1	⊠	5-1/4"	7-1/4"	9-1/4"

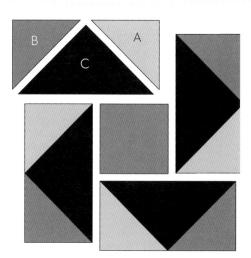

Flying Geese from Triangles—page 16
Partial Seams—page 20

Nine Patch

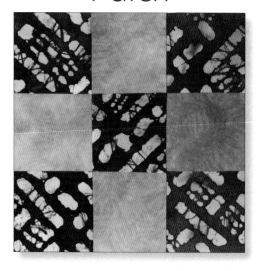

Color/Cut		Subcut	6"	9"	12"
A	4		2-1/2"	3-1/2"	4-1/2"
B	5		2-1/2"	3-1/2"	4-1/2"

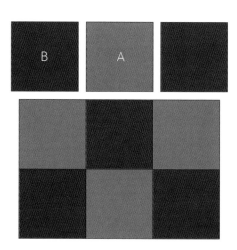

This nine patch is a simple beginner block, good for practicing accurate seams.

Nine Patch Variation

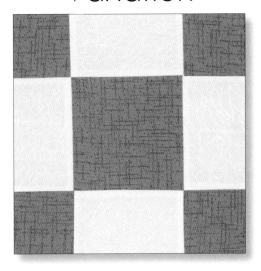

Color/Cut		Subcut	6"	9"	12"
A	4	▭	2" x 3-1/2"	2-3/4" x 5"	3-1/2" x 6-1/2"
B	1	▪	3-1/2"	5"	6-1/2"
B	4	▪	2"	2-3/4"	3-1/2"

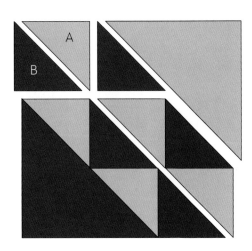

A Nine Patch can have unequal sized pieces as long as it has nine parts. (See Nine Patch page 65.)

North Wind

Color/Cut		Subcut	6"	9"	12"
A	1	◹	4-7/8"	6-7/8"	8-7/8"
A	3	◹	2-7/8"	3-7/8"	4-7/8"
B	1	◹	4-7/8"	6-7/8"	8-7/8"
B	3	◹	2-7/8"	3-7/8"	4-7/8"

There will be triangles left over from A & B HST subcuts.

Triangles-in-a-Row—pages 26-27

Ohio Star

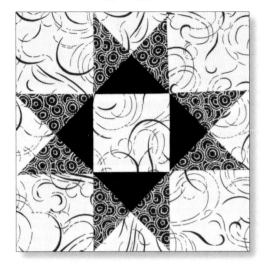

Color/Cut		Subcut	6"	9"	12"
A	5	☐	2-1/2"	3-1/2"	4-1/2"
A	1	☐ ⊠	3-1/4"	4-1/4"	5-1/4"
B	2	⊠	3-1/4"	4-1/4"	5-1/4"
C	1	⊠	3-1/4"	4-1/4"	5-1/4"

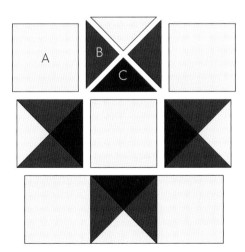

QST—page 14

Old Maid's Puzzle

Color/Cut		Subcut	6"	9"	12"
A	3	◩ ◸	2-7/8"	3-7/8"	4-7/8"
B	3	◼ ◸	2-7/8"	3-7/8"	4-7/8"
B	3	◼	2-1/2"	3-1/2"	4-1/2"

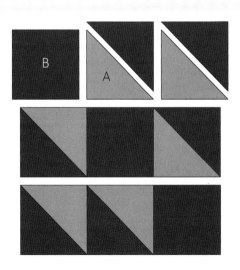

HST—pages 12-13

Puss In
The Corner

Color/Cut		Subcut	6"	9"	12"
A	1		4-1/2"	6-1/2"	8-1/2""
B	2	◻	1-7/8"	2-3/8"	2-7/8"
C	2	◻	1-7/8"	2-3/8"	2-7/8""
C	4		1-1/2" x 4-1/2"	2" x 6-1/2"	2-1/2" x 8-1/2"

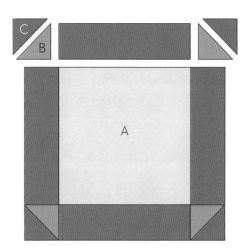

HST—pages 12-13; This could be a great setting block to alternate with more intricate 3 and 6 grid blocks.

Rail
Fence

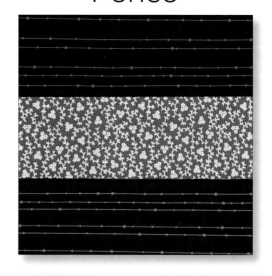

Color/Cut		Subcut	6"	9"	12"
A	2		2-1/2" x 6-1/2"	3-1/2" x 9-1/2"	4-1/2" x 12-1/2"
B	1		2-1/2" x 6-1/2"	3-1/2" x 9-1/2"	4-1/2" x 12-1/2"

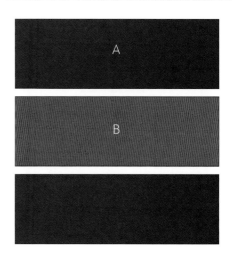

It's a simple block. Alternate blocks horizontally and vertically for an easy, quick quilt.

Ribbon Quilt

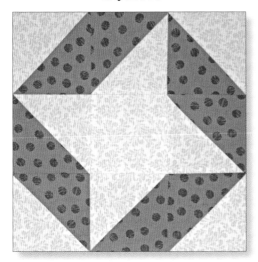

Color/Cut		Subcut	6"	9"	12"
A	1		2-1/2"	3-1/2"	4-1/2"
A	4	◹	2-7/8"	3-7/8"	4-7/8"
B	4	◹	2-7/8"	3-7/8"	4-7/8"

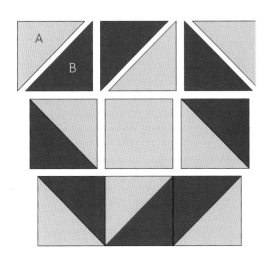

HST—pages 12-13
Pay attention to the orientation of HSTs when sewing this block together.

Rocky Road To California

Color/Cut		Subcut	6"	9"	12"
A	2	◹	2-7/8"	3-7/8"	4-7/8"
B	2	◹	2-7/8"	3-7/8"	4-7/8"
B	6		1-1/2"	2"	2-1/2"
C	6		1-1/2"	2"	2-1/2"
C	2		2-1/2"	3-1/2"	4-1/2"

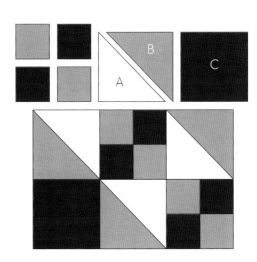

HST—pages 12-13

Rolling Stone Block

Color/Cut		Subcut	6"	9"	12"
A	5		2-1/2"	3-1/2"	4-1/2"
A	4		1-1/2" x 2-1/2"	2" x 3-1/2"	2-1/2" x 4-1/2"
B	4		1-1/2" x 2-1/2"	2" x 3-1/2"	2-1/2" x 4-1/2"
B	16		1-1/2"	2"	2-1/2"

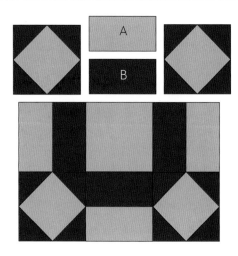

Square-in-a-Square—page 23

Roundabout Block

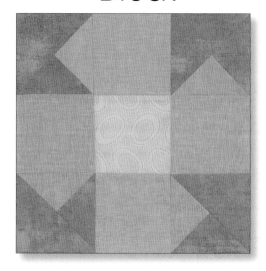

Color/Cut		Subcut	6"	9"	12"
A	1		2-1/2"	3-1/2"	4-1/2"
B	1	⊠	3-1/4"	4-1/4"	5-1/4"
C	1	⊠	3-1/4"	4-1/4"	5-1/4"
C	2	◻	2-7/8"	3-7/8"	4-7/8"

Block designed by Sue Voegtlin

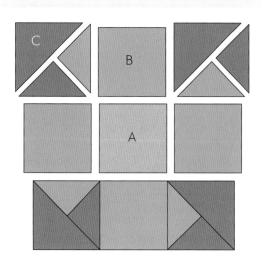

HST—pages 12-13
QST—page 14 (steps 1-4)

Sail Boat

Color/Cut		Subcut	6"	9"	12"
A	3	◺	2-7/8"	3-7/8"	4-7/8"
A	1	◺	4-7/8"	6-7/8"	8-7/8"
B	4	◺	2-7/8"	3-7/8"	4-7/8"
C	1		2-1/2"	3-1/2"	4-1/2"

There will be triangles left over from A & B HST subcuts.

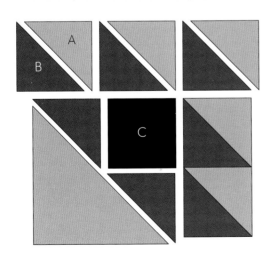

HST—pages 12-13
Adding Triangles to a Square—page 25

Split Nine Patch

Color/Cut		Subcut	6"	9"	12"
A	2	▢	2-1/2"	3-1/2"	4-1/2"
A	3	◺	2-7/8"	3-7/8"	4-7/8"
B	1	◼	2-1/2"	3-1/2"	4-1/2"
B	3	◺	2-7/8"	3-7/8"	4-7/8"

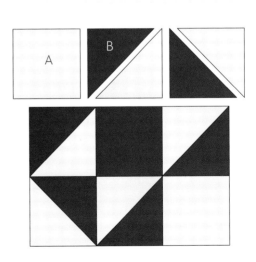

HST—pages 12-13

Sunset Light

Color/Cut	Subcut	6"	9"	12"
A	2	2-1/2"	3-1/2"	4-1/2"
A	2	1-1/2" x 2-1/2"	2" x 3-1/2"	2-1/2" x 4-1/2"
B	4	2-1/2"	3-1/2"	4-1/2"
C	4	1-1/2"	2"	2-1/2"
D	4	1-1/2"	2"	2-1/2"

Block designed by Laurel Albright

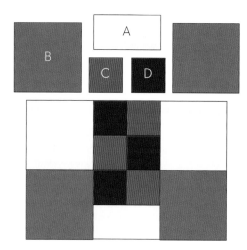

Try using solid colors for the components in this block. Experiment with your favorite colors for a more contemporary look.

The Letter X

Color/Cut	Subcut	6"	9"	12"
A	3	⊠	3-1/4"	4-1/4"	5-1/4"
B	3	⊠	3-1/4"	4-1/4"	5-1/4"
C	4		2-1/2"	3-1/2"	4-1/2"

There will be triangles left over from A & B QST subcuts.

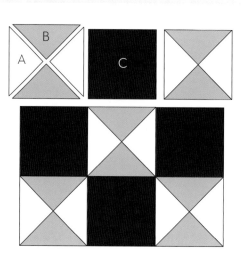

QST—pages 14-15

72

The Practical Orchard

Color/Cut		Subcut	6"	9"	12"
A	2		2-1/2"	3-1/2"	4-1/2"
A	2	◻	2-7/8"	3-7/8"	4-7/8"
A	1	⊠	3-1/4"	4-1/4"	5-1/4"
B	2		2-1/2"	3-1/2"	4-1/2"
B	2	◻	2-7/8"	3-7/8"	4-7/8"
B	1	⊠	3-1/4"	4-1/4"	5-1/4"

There will be triangles left over from A & B QST subcuts.

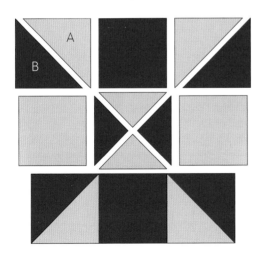

HST—pages 12-13
QST—page 14

The Railroad

Color/Cut		Subcut	6"	9"	12"
A	10		1-1/2"	2"	2-1/2"
A	2	◻	2-7/8"	3-7/8"	4-7/8"
B	10		1-1/2"	2"	2-1/2"
C	2	◻	2-7/8"	3-7/8"	4-7/8"

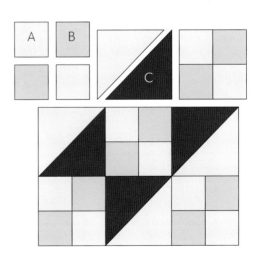

HST—pages 12-13

Three and Six Block

Color/Cut		Subcut	6"	9"	12"
A	2	◹	2-7/8"	3-7/8"	4-7/8"
B	1	◹	2-7/8"	3-7/8"	4-7/8"
B	1		2-1/2"	3-1/2"	4-1/2"
C	2		2-1/2"	3-1/2"	4-1/2"
D	3	◹	2-7/8"	3-7/8"	4-7/8"

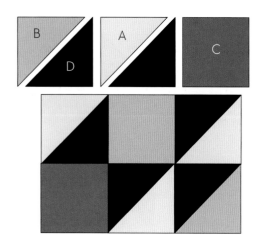

HST—pages 12-13

Toy Windmill

Color/Cut		Subcut	6"	9"	12"
A	2		1-1/2" x 2-1/2"	2" x 3-1/2"	2-1/2" x 4-1/2"
A	2	◹	1-7/8"	2-3/8"	2-7/8"
A	2		2-1/2" x 3-1/2"	3-1/2" x 5"	4-1/2" x 6-1/2"
A	2		2-1/2"	3-1/2"	4-1/2"
B	2	◹	1-7/8"	2-3/8"	2-7/8"
B	4		1-1/2" x 2-1/2"	2" x 3-1/2"	2-1/2" x 4-1/2"

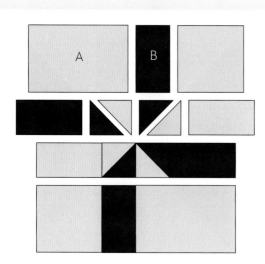

HST—pages 12-13

74

Twin Sisters

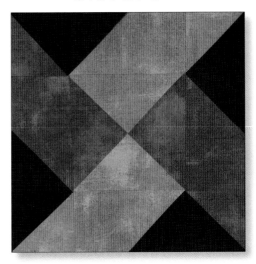

Color/Cut		Subcut	6"	9"	12"
A	1	◻	3-7/8"	5-3/8"	6-7/8"
*A	2		2" x 3-1/2"	2-3/4" x 5"	3-1/2" x 6-1/2"
A	1	◻	2-3/8"	3-1/8"	3-7/8""
B	1	◻	3-7/8"	5-3/8"	6-7/8"
*B	2		2" x 3-1/2"	2-3/4" x 5"	3-1/2" x 6-1/2"
B	1	◻	2-3/8"	3-1/8"	3-7/8"
C	2	◻	2-3/8"	3-1/8"	3-7/8"
*C	4		2"	2-3/4"	3-1/2"

*For Adding Corners, page 24, use rectangles and 4-C squares.

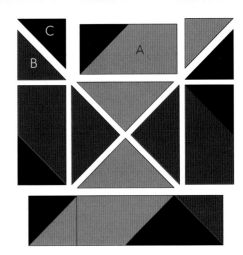

QST—page 14
Adding Corners—page 24

Twin Star

Color/Cut		Subcut	6"	9"	12"
A	5	◻	2-1/2"	3-1/2"	4-1/2"
A	1	◻ ⊠	3-1/4"	4-1/4"	5-1/4"
B	1	◻ ⊠	3-1/4"	4-1/4"	5-1/4"
C	2	◻ ◻	2-7/8"	3-7/8"	4-7/8"

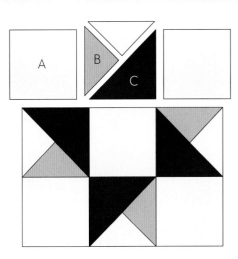

HST—pages 12-13
QST—page 14 (steps 1-4)

The 4 x 4 Grid Blocks

The 4 x 4 grid is really interesting to me; more squares = more detail. Half-square triangles are used repeatedly in many of the blocks. But patterns made by turning, flipping, and repeating them give the blocks a personality of their own. Half-square triangles can make flying geese and pinwheels. It's all in the way they are oriented.

Aircraft Block

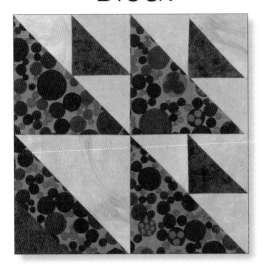

Color/Cut		Subcut	6"	9"	12"
A	1	◻	3-7/8"	5-3/8"	6-7/8"
A	5	◻	2-3/8"	3-1/8"	3-7/8"
B	2	◻	3-7/8"	5-3/8"	6-7/8"
C	2	◻	2-3/8"	3-1/8"	3-7/8"
*C	1		2"	2-3/4"	3-1/2"

*Add the C square to the corner of the HST, lower left.

There will be triangles left over from A & C HST subcuts.

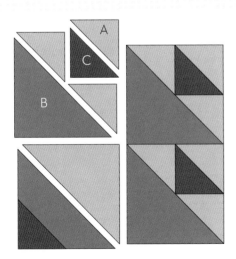

HST—pages 12-13
Adding Triangles to a Square—page 25
Adding Corners—page 24

Angela's Star

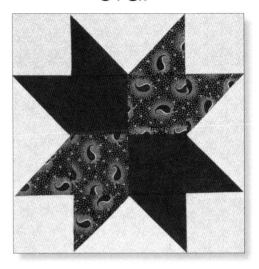

Color/Cut		Subcut	6"	9"	12"
A	4	◻	2"	2-3/4"	3-1/2"
*A	4	▭	2" x 3-1/2"	2-3/4" x 5"	3-1/2" x 6-1/2"
*B	6	◼	2"	2-3/4"	3-1/2"
*C	6	◼	2"	2-3/4"	3-1/2"

*Use 4-B & C squares, and 4-A rectangles to make Flying Geese from Squares, page 17.

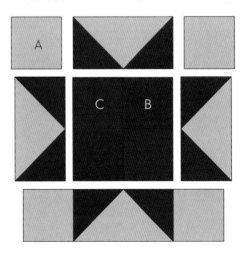

Flying Geese from Squares—page 17

Bachelor's Puzzle

Color/Cut		Subcut	6"	9"	12"
A	4		2"	2-3/4"	3-1/2"
B	1		3-1/2'''	5"	6-1/2"
*C	4		2" x 3-1/2"	2-3/4" x 5"	3-1/2" x 6-1/2"
*D	12		2"	2-3/4"	3-1/2"

*Use C rectangles and 8-D squares to make parallel blocks, page 22.

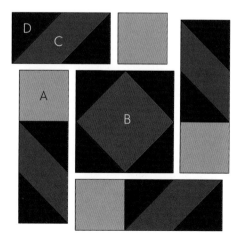

Parallel Seams—page 22
Square-in-a-Square—page 23

Balkan Puzzle

Color/Cut		Subcut	6"	9"	12"
*A	4		2"	2-3/4"	3-1/2"
A	2	◻	2-3/8"	3-1/8"	3-7/8"
*B	4		2" x 3-1/2"	2-3/4" x 5"	3-1/2" x 6-1/2"
C	2	◻	2-3/8"	3-1/8"	3-7/8"
*C	8		2"	2-3/4"	3-1/2"
C	1		3-1/2"	5"	6-1/2"

*Use 4-A & C squares, and 4-B rectangles to make Flying Geese from Squares, page 17.

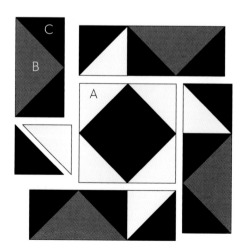

HST—pages 12-13
Flying Geese from Squares—page 17
Square-in-a-Square—page 23

Brave World

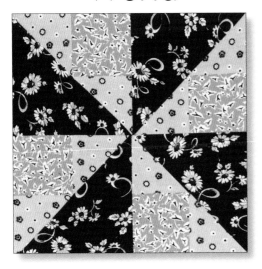

Color/Cut		Subcut	6"	9"	12"
A	4		2-7/8"	3-1/8"	3-7/8"
B	4		2"	2-3/4"	3-1/2"
C	2		3-7/8"	5-3/8"	6-7/8"

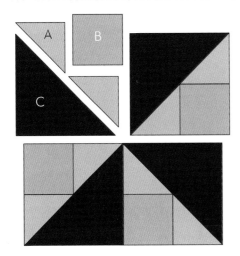

HST—pages 12-13
Adding Triangles to a Square—page 25

Brown Goose

Color/Cut		Subcut	6"	9"	12"
*A	1		4-1/4"	5-3/4"	7-1/4"
**A	4		2-3/8"	3-1/8"	3-7/8"
**B	1		4-1/4"	5-3/4"	7-1/4"
*B	4		2-3/8"	3-1/8"	3-7/8"

* Use the large A square and 4-B squares to make Four-at-a-Time Flying Geese, page 18.

**Use the large B square and 4-A squares to make Four-at-a-Time Flying Geese, page 18.

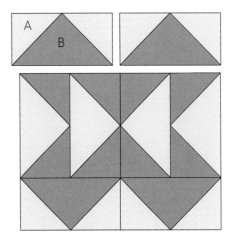

Four-at-a-Time Flying Geese—page 18

Cheyenne Block

Color/Cut		Subcut	6"	9"	12"
A	1 ▢		3-1/2"	5"	6-1/2"
A	2 ▢	◺	2-3/8"	3-1/8"	3-7/8"
B	6 ◼		2"	2-3/4"	3-1/2"
B	1 ◼	◺	2-3/8"	3-1/8"	3-7/8"
C	6 ◼		2"	2-3/4"	3-1/2"
C	1 ◼	◺	2-3/8"	3-1/8"	3-7/8""

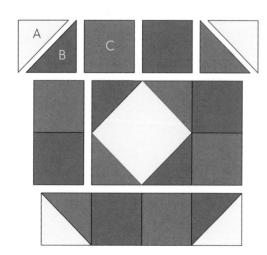

HST—pages 12-13
Square-in-a-Square—page 23

Clay's Choice

Color/Cut		Subcut	6"	9"	12"
A	4 ▢		2"	2-3/4"	3-1/2"
A	4 ▢	◺	2-3/8"	3-1/8"	3-7/8"
B	4 ◼		2"	2-3/4"	3-1/2"
C	4 ◼	◺	2-3/8"	3-1/8"	3-7/8"

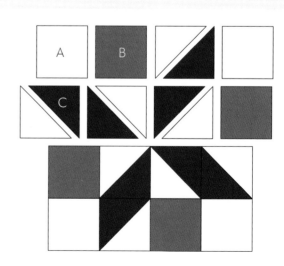

HST—pages 12-13

Clay's Choice Variation

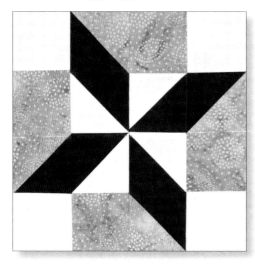

Color/Cut		Subcut	6"	9"	12"
A	4 ▫		2"	2-3/4"	3-1/2"
A	2 ▫	◺	2-3/8"	3-1/8"	3-7/8"
B	4 ▪		2"	2-3/4"	3-1/2"
B	2 ▪	◺	2-3/8"	3-1/8"	3-7/8"
C	4 ▪	◺	2-3/8"	3-1/8"	3-7/8"

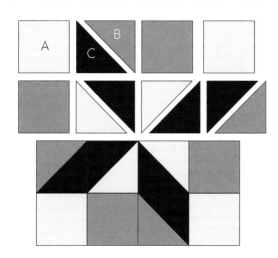

HST—pages 12-13

Colorado Beauty

Color/Cut		Subcut	6"	9"	12"
A	4 ▫	◺	2-3/8"	3-1/8"	3-7/8"
*A	1 ▫		4-1/4"	5-3/4"	7-1/4"
*B	4 ▪		2-3/8"	3-1/8"	3-7/8"
B	4 ▪	◺	2-3/8"	3-1/8"	3-7/8"

*Use the large A square and 4-B squares to make Four-at-a-Time Flying Geese, page 18.

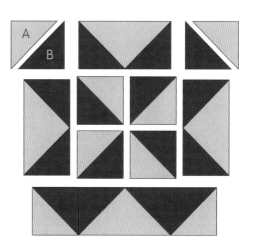

HST—pages 12-13
Four-at-a-Time Flying Geese—page 18

Crossed Paths

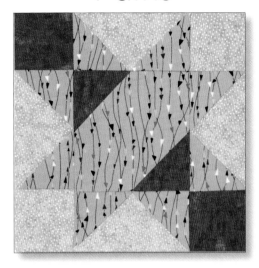

Color/Cut		Subcut	6"	9"	12"
**A	1		3-1/2"	5"	6-1/2"
*A	4		2-3/8"	3-1/8"	3-7/8"
*B	1		4-1/4"	5-3/4"	7-1/2"
B	2		2"	2-3/4"	3-1/2"
**C	4		2"	2-3/4"	3-1/2"

*Use the large B square and 4-A squares to make Four-at-a-Time Flying Geese, page 18.

**For Adding Corners, page 24, use large A block and 2-C blocks.

Block designed by Sue Voegtlin

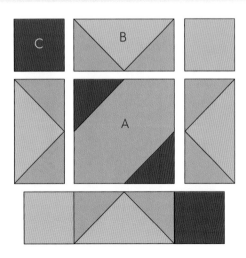

Four-at-a-Time Flying Geese—page 18
Adding Corners—page 24

Double Four-Patch

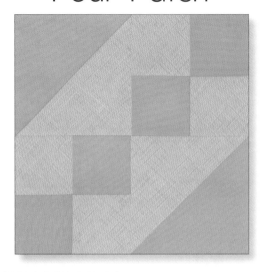

Color/Cut		Subcut	6"	9"	12"
A	1	◹	3-7/8"	5-3/8"	6-7/8"
A	4		2"	2-3/4"	3-1/2"
B	1	◹	3-7/8"	5-3/8"	6-7/8"
B	4		2"	2-3/4"	3-1/2"

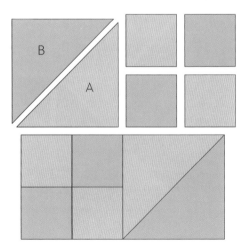

HST—pages 12-13

Double Quartet

Color/Cut		Subcut	6"	9"	12"
A	4 ▢		2"	2-3/4"	3-1/2"
A	4 ▢	◹	2-3/8"	3-1/8"	3-7/8"
B	4 ■		2"	2-3/4"	3-1/2"
B	4 ■	◹	2-3/8"	3-1/8"	3-7/8"

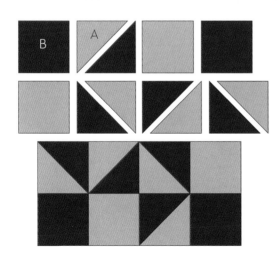

HST—pages 12-13

Dutchman's Puzzle

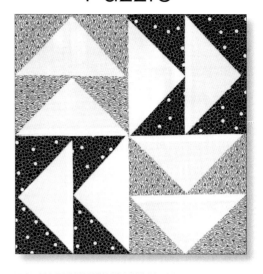

Color/Cut		Subcut	6"	9"	12"
*A	2 ▢		4-1/4"	5-3/4"	7-1/4"
*B	4 ▢		2-3/8"	3-1/8"	3-7/8"
*C	4 ■		2-3/8"	3-1/8"	3-7/8"

Note: The 2-A squares are for "geese" bodies and the B & C squares are for "sky" to make Four-at-a-Time Flying Geese, page 18.

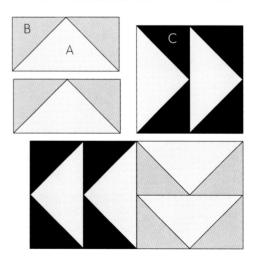

Four-at-a-Time Flying Geese—page 18

Fancy Corners

Color/Cut		Subcut	6"	9"	12"
*A	1 ☐		3-1/2"	5"	6-1/2"
A	4 ☐		2"	2-3/4"	3-1/2"
A	3 ☐	◻	2-3/8"	3-1/8"	3-7/8"
B	1 ◧	⊠	2-3/4"	3-1/2"	4-1/4"
C	1 ◧	⊠	2-3/4"	3-1/2"	4-1/4"
*D	2 ◧		2"	2-3/4"	3-1/2"
D	4 ◧	◻	2-3/8"	3-1/8"	3-7/8"

For Adding Corners, page 24, use large A square and 2-D squares. There will be triangles left over from B & C QST subcuts.

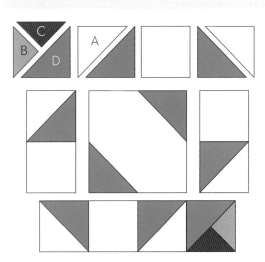

HST—pages 12-13
QST—page 14 (steps 1-4)
Adding Corners—page 24

Fishing Boats

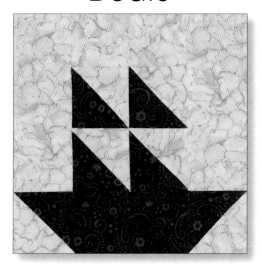

Color/Cut		Subcut	6"	9"	12"
A	3 ☐	◻	2-3/8"	3-1/8"	3-7/8"
A	1 ☐		2" x 3-1/2"	2-3/4" x 5"	3-1/2" x 6-1/2"
A	2 ☐		2" X 5"	2-3/4" X 7-1/4"	3-1/2" X 9-1/2"
B	1 ■		2" x 3-1/2"	2-3/4" x 5"	3-1/2" x 6-1/2"
B	3 ■	◻	2-3/8"	3-1/8"	3-7/8"

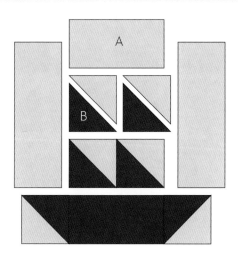

HST—pages 12-13

Flower Basket

Color/Cut		Subcut	6"	9"	12"
A	4		2-3/8"	3-1/8"	3-7/8"
B	2		2" x 3-1/2"	2-3/4" x 5"	3-1/2" x 6-1/2"
B	1		2"	2-3/4"	3-1/2"
B	1		2-3/8"	3-1/8"	3-7/8"
C	1		2"	2-3/4"	3-1/2"
C	3		2-3/8"	3-1/8"	3-7/8"
D	2		2-3/8"	3-1/8"	3-7/8"

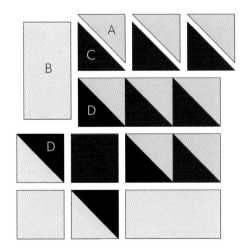

HST—pages 12-13

Four by Four Block

Color/Cut		Subcut	6"	9"	12"
A	4		2"	2-3/4"	3-1/2"
B	1		6-1/2"	9-1/2"	12-1/2"
C	4		2-3/8"	3-1/8"	3-7/8"

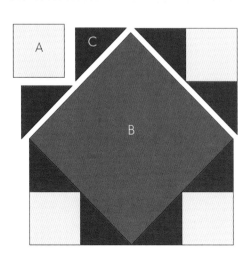

Adding Triangles to a Square—page 25

Free Trade

Color/Cut		Subcut	6"	9"	12"
*A	4 ▭		4-1/4"	5-3/4"	7-1/4"
A	6 ☐		2"	2-3/4"	3-1/2"
A	1 ☐	◪	2-3/8"	3-1/8"	3-7/8"
B	1 ◼	◪	2-3/8"	3-1/8"	3-7/8"
*B	8 ◼		2"	2-3/4"	3-1/2"

*Use the A rectangles and B squares to make Flying Geese from Squares, page 17.

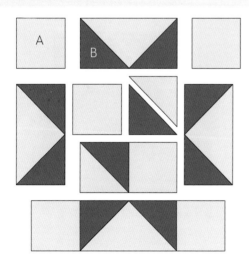

HST—pages 12-13
Flying Geese from Squares—page 17

Girl's Favorite

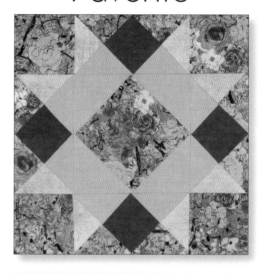

Color/Cut		Subcut	6"	9"	12"
A	2 ☐	⊠	2-3/4"	3-1/2"	4-1/4"
B	2 ▦	⊠	2-3/4"	3-1/2"	4-1/4"
B	4 ▦		2"	2-3/4"	3-1/2"
C	2 ◼	⊠	2-3/4"	3-1/2"	4-1/4"
C	1 ◼		3-1/2"	5"	6-1/2"
C	4 ◼		2"	2-3/4"	3-1/2"
D	2 ◼	⊠	2-3/4"	3-1/2"	4-1/4"

Note: There are 41 pieces in this block. Have no fear! Just lay out the pieces before you start sewing.

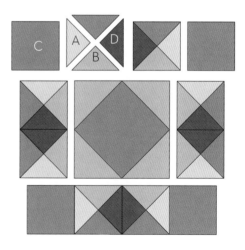

QST—page 14
Square-in-a-Square—page 23

Indian Hatchet

Color/Cut		Subcut	6"	9"	12"
A	2		2"	2-3/4"	3-1/2"
A	4	◿	2-3/8"	3-1/8"	3-7/8"
B	1		3-1/2"	5"	6-1/2"
C	4	◿	2-3/8"	3-1/8"	3-7/8"
C	2		2"	2-3/4"	3-1/2"

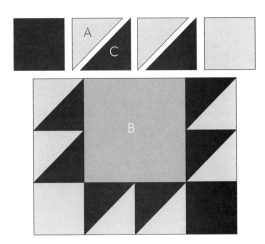

HST—pages 12-13

Jack in the Box

Color/Cut		Subcut	6"	9"	12"
*A	6		2" X 3-1/2"	2-3/4" X 5"	3-1/2" X 6-1/2"
A	2	◿	2-3/8"	3-1/8"	3-7/8"
B	2	◿	2-3/8"	3-1/8"	3-7/8"
*B	12		2"	2-3/4"	3-1/2"

*Use A rectangles and B squares to make Flying Geese from Squares on page 17.

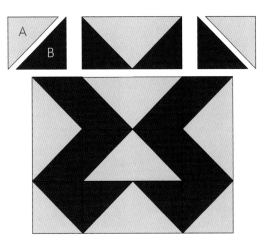

HST—pages 12-13
Flying Geese from Squares—page 17

Marion's Choice

Color/Cut		Subcut	6"	9"	12"
A	1	☐ ⊠	4-1/4"	5-3/4"	7-1/4"
A	2	☐ ◺	2-3/8"	3-1/8"	3-7/8"
A	2	☐ ⊠	2-3/4"	3-1/2"	4-1/4"
B	1	◼ ⊠	4-1/4"	5-3/4"	7-1/4"
B	2	◼ ◺	2-3/8"	3-1/8"	3-7/8"
B	1	◼ ⊠	2-3/4"	3-1/2"	4-1/4"

Note: Referring to illustration below and paying close attention to color orientation, make QSTs first. Add small A and B triangles to two sides of each QST. Add large A/B triangle sets to finish the "square."

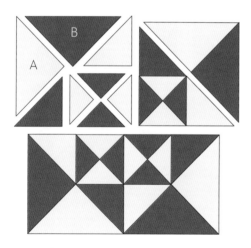

HST—pages 12-13
QST—pages 14-15
Adding Triangles to a Square—page 25

Mill Wheel Block

Color/Cut		Subcut	6"	9"	12"
A	8	◻	2"	2-3/4"	3-1/2"
A	4	◻ ◺	2-3/8"	3-1/8"	3-7/8"
B	4	◼ ◺	2-3/8"	3-1/8"	3-7/8"
C	1	◼	3-1/2"	5"	6-1/2"

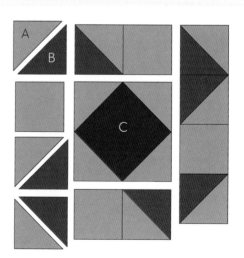

HST—pages 12-13
Square-in-a-Square—page 23

Mosaic 6 Block

Color/Cut		Subcut	6"	9"	12"
A	1		3-1/2"	5"	6-1/2"
A	6	◹	2-3/8"	3-1/8"	3-7/8"
B	6	◹	2-3/8"	3-1/8"	3-7/8"
B	4		2"	2-3/4"	3-1/2"

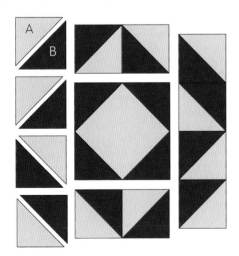

HST—pages 12-13
Square-in-a-Square—page 23

Mosaic 9 Block

Color/Cut		Subcut	6"	9"	12"
A	8	◹	2-3/8"	3-1/8"	3-7/8"
B	4	◹	2-3/8"	3-1/8"	3-7/8"
C	4	◹	2-3/8"	3-1/8"	3-7/8"

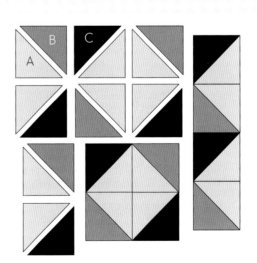

HST—pages 12-13

Mosaic 10 Block

Color/Cut		Subcut	6"	9"	12"
*A	8	▢	2"	2-3/4"	3-1/2"
*A	2	▭	2" x 3-1/2"	2-3/4" x 5"	3-1/2" x 6-1/2"
B	1	▢	3-1/2"	5"	6-1/2"
C	4	▢	2"	2-3/4"	3-1/2""
*D	4	▭	2" x 3-1/2"	2-3/4" x 5"	3-1/2" x 6-1/2"
*D	4	▢	2"	2-3/4"	3-1/2"

*Use 8-A squares/4-D rectangles, and 2-A rectangles/4-D squares to make Flying Geese from Squares, page 17.

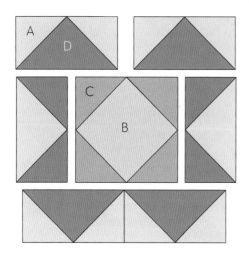

Flying Geese from Squares—page 17
Square-in-a-Square—page 23

Mosaic 12 Block

Color/Cut		Subcut	6"	9"	12"
*A	8	▢	2-3/8"	3-1/8"	3-7/8"
*B	1	▢	4-1/4"	5-3/4"	7-1/4"
*C	1	▢	4-1/4"	5-3/4"	7-1/4"

Note: Use B & C squares for "geese" bodies and A squares are for "sky" to make Four-at-a-Time Flying Geese, page 18.

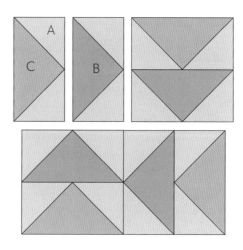

Four-at-a-Time Flying Geese—page 18

Mosaic 13 Block

Color/Cut		Subcut	6"	9"	12"
*A	4 ▢		2"	2-3/4"	3-1/2"
A	2 ▢	◸	2-3/8"	3-1/8"	3-7/8"
B	2 ◼	◸	2-3/8"	3-1/8"	3-7/8"
*B	4 ◼		2"	2-3/4"	3-1/2"
*C	4 ▭		2" x 3-1/2"	2-3/4" x 5"	3-1/2" x 6-1/2"
D	2 ◼	◸	2-3/8"	3-1/8"	3-7/8"
E	2 ◼	◸	2-3/8"	3-1/8"	3-7/8"

*Use A & B squares and C rectangles to make Flying Geese from Squares, page 17.

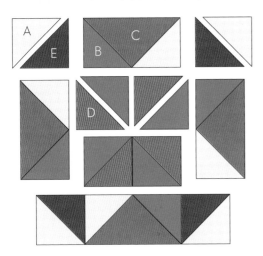

HST—pages 12-13
Flying Geese From Squares—page 17
Geese have light and dark "sky" triangles.

Mosaic 13 Variation

Color/Cut		Subcut	6"	9"	12"
*A	4 ▢		2"	2-3/4"	3-1/2"
A	2 ▢	◸	2-3/8"	3-1/8"	3-7/8"
B	4 ◼		2"	2-3/4"	3-1/2"
*C	4 ▭		2" x 3-1/2"	2-3/4" x 5"	3-1/2" x 6-1/2"
*D	4 ◼		2"	2-3/4"	3-1/2"
D	2 ◼	◸	2-3/8"	3-1/8"	3-7/8"

*Use A & D squares and C rectangles to make Flying Geese from Squares, page 17.

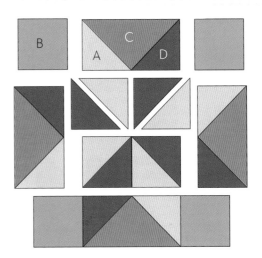

HST—pages 12-13
Flying Geese From Squares—page 17
Geese have light and dark "sky" triangles.

Mosaic 17 Block

Color/Cut		Subcut	6"	9"	12"
A	8 ⬜	◻	2-3/8"	3-1/8"	3-7/8"
B	8 ◼	◻	2-3/8"	3-1/8"	3-7/8"
	assorted colors				

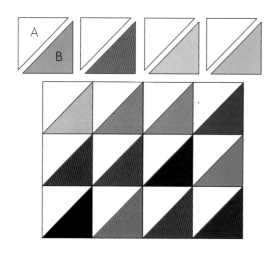

HST—pages 12-13
This is a good block to use up scraps and experiment with your own color combinations.

Mosaic 18 Block

Color/Cut		Subcut	6"	9"	12"
*A	8 ◻		2"	2-3/4"	3-1/2"
A	2 ◻	◻	2-3/8"	3-1/8"	3-7/8"
B	2 ◻	◻	2-3/8"	3-1/8"	3-7/8"
C	4 ◻	◻	2-3/8"	3-1/8"	3-7/8"
*D	4 ◼		2" x 3-1/2"	2-3/4" x 5"	3-1/2" x 6-1/2"

*Use A squares and D rectangles to make Parallel Seams, page 22.

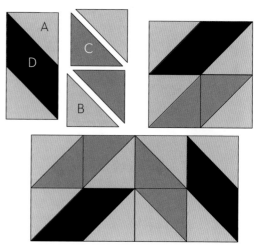

HST—pages 12-13
Parallel Seams—page 22

Mosaic 20 Block

Color/Cut		Subcut	6"	9"	12"
A	2	◧	2-3/8"	3-1/8"	3-7/8"
A	1		3-1/2"	5"	6-1/2"
*A	8		2"	2-3/4"	3-1/2"
B	2	◧	2-3/8"	3-1/8"	3-7/8"
B	4		2"	2-3/4"	3-1/2"
*B	4		2" x 3-1/2"	2-3/4" x 5"	3-1/2" x 6-1/2"

*Use A squares and B rectangles to make Flying Geese from Squares, page 17.

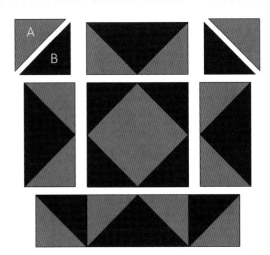

HST—pages 12-13
Flying Geese from Squares—page 17
Square-in-a-Square—page 23

Mosaic 21 Block

Color/Cut		Subcut	6"	9"	12"
A	1		3-1/2"	5"	6-1/2"
A	6	◧	2-3/8"	3-1/8"	3-7/8"
B	2		2"	2-3/4"	3-1/2"
B	2	◧	2-3/8"	3-1/8"	3-7/8"
C	2		2"	2-3/4"	3-1/2"
C	2	◧	2-3/8"	3-1/8"	3-7/8"
D	2	◧	2-3/8"	3-1/8"	3-7/8"

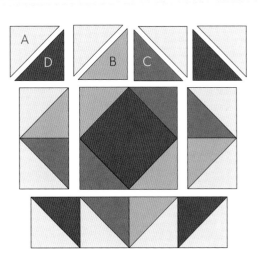

HST—pages 12-13
Square-in-a-Square—page 23

Mr. Roosevelt's Necktie

Color/Cut		Subcut	6"	9"	12"
A	1		3-1/2"	5"	6-1/2"
A	4		2"	2-3/4"	3-1/2"
B	6		2"	2-3/4"	3-1/2"
C	6		2"	2-3/4"	3-1/2"

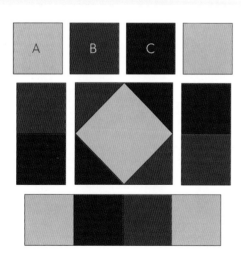

Square-in-a-Square—page 23

Navajo Block

Color/Cut		Subcut	6"	9"	12"
A	2		2"	2-3/4"	3-1/2"
A	5	◻	2-3/8"	3-1/8"	3-7/8"
B	2		1-1/4"- 3-1/2"	1-5/8" x 5"	2" x 6-1/2"
B	2		1-1/4" x 2"	1-5/8" x 2-3/4"	2" x 3-1/2"
C	1		2"	2-3/4"	3-1/2"
D	5	◻	2-3/8"	3-1/8"	3-7/8"

The "C" square was fussy cut from striped fabric.

For "D" squares use assorted colors.

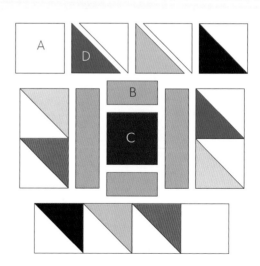

HST—pages 12-13

Old
Tippecanoe

Color/Cut		Subcut	6"	9"	12"
A	8		2-3/8"	3-1/8"	3-7/8"
B	4		2-3/8"	3-1/8"	3-7/8"
C	4		2-3/8"	3-1/8"	3-7/8"

HST—pages 12-13

Our
Editor

Color/Cut		Subcut	6"	9"	12"
A	2		2-3/8"	3-1/8"	3-7/8"
*A	2		2" x 3-1/2"	2-3/4" x 5"	3-1/2" x 6-1/2"
*A	8		2"	2-3/4"	3-1/2"
B	2		2-3/8"	3-1/8"	3-7/8"
*B	4		2" x 3-1/2"	2-3/4" x 5"	3-1/2" x 6-1/2"
*B	4		2"	2-3/4"	3-1/2"

*Use A squares/B rectangles, and B squares/A rectangles to make Flying Geese from Squares, page 17.

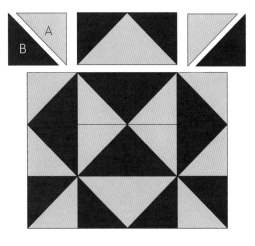

HST—pages 12-13
Flying Geese from Squares—page 17

Pale Stars

Color/Cut		Subcut	6"	9"	12"
*A	8	▫	2"	2-3/4"	3-1/2"
*B	4	▪	2"	2-3/4"	3-1/2"
*C	4	▬	2" x 3-1/2"	2-3/4" x 5"	3-1/2" x 6-1/2"
D	4	■	2"	2-3/4"	3-1/2"

*Use 4-A squares, 4-B squares and 4-C rectangles to make Flying Geese from Squares, page 17.

Note: The center can also be cut as a square; 3-1/2", 5" or 6-1/2".

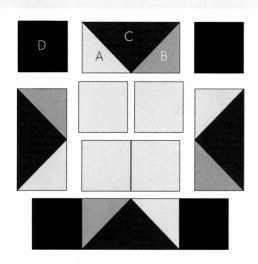

Flying Geese From Squares—page 17

Path Through the Woods

Color/Cut		Subcut	6"	9"	12"
A	1	◹	5-3/8"	7-5/8"	9-7/8"
A	4	◹	2-3/8"	3-1/8"	3-7/8"
B	1	◹	5-3/8"	7-5/8"	9-7/8"
B	4	◹	2-3/8"	3-1/8"	3-7/8"

There will be triangles left over from A & B HST subcuts.

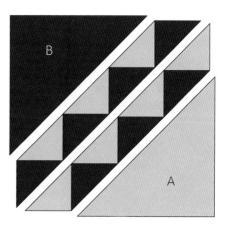

HST—pages 12-13
Triangles-in-a-Row—page 26

Patience Corners

Color/Cut		Subcut	6"	9"	12"
A	4 ☐		2"	2-3/4"	3-1/2"
A	2 ☐	◹	2-3/8"	3-1/8"	3-7/8"
B	4 ☐		2"	2-3/4"	3-1/2"
B	2 ☐	◹	2-3/8"	3-1/8"	3-7/8"
C	2 ☐		3-1/2"	5"	6-1/2"
C	4 ☐	◹	2-3/8"	3-1/8"	3-7/8"

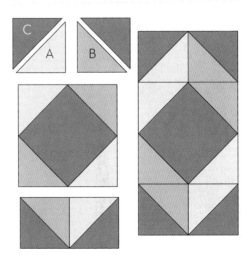

HST—pages 12-13
Square-in-a-Square—page 23

Pinwheel Block

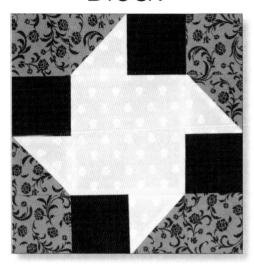

Color/Cut		Subcut	6"	9"	12"
A	1 ☐		3-1/2"	5"	6-1/2"
A	2 ☐	◹	2-3/8"	3-1/8"	3-7/8"
B	4 ☐		2"	2-3/4"	3-1/2"
B	2 ☐	◹	2-3/8"	3-1/8"	3-7/8"
C	4 ☐		2"	2-3/4"	3-1/2"

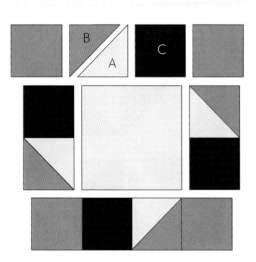

HST—pages 12-13

Red and White Cross

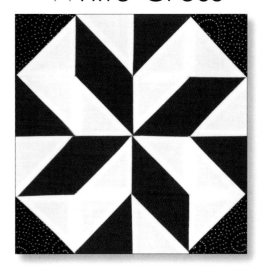

Color/Cut		Subcut	6"	9"	12"
A	8 ⬜	◺	2-3/8"	3-1/8"	3-7/8"
B	6 ⬛	◺	2-3/8"	3-1/8"	3-7/8"
C	2 ⬛	◺	2-3/8"	3-1/8"	3-7/8"

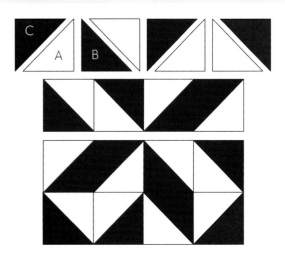

HST—pages 12-13

Ribbon Border

Color/Cut		Subcut	6"	9"	12"
A	1 🟦	⊠	4-1/4"	5-3/4"	7-1/4"
A	2 🟦	⊠	2-3/8"	3-1/8"	3-7/8"
B	2 🟦	⊠	2-3/8"	3-1/8"	3-7/8"
B	2 🟦	◺	3-7/8"	5-3/8"	6-7/8"

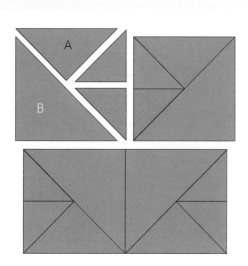

HST—pages 12-13
QST—page 14 (steps 1-4)

Road to Oklahoma

Color/Cut		Subcut	6"	9"	12"
A	6		2"	2-3/4"	3-1/2"
A	2	◺	2-3/8"	3-1/8"	3-7/8"
B	4		2"	2-3/4"	3-1/2"
B	2	◺	2-3/8"	3-1/8"	3-7/8"
C	2		2"	2-3/4"	3-1/2"

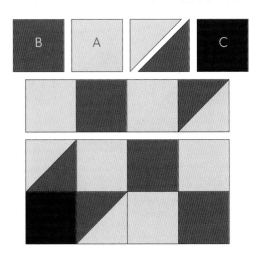

HST—pages 12-13

Scrap Zig Zag

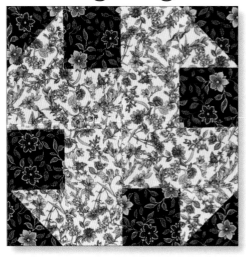

Color/Cut		Subcut	6"	9"	12"
A	4		2" x 3-1/2"	2-3/4" x 5"	3-1/2" x 6-1/2"
A	2	◺	2-3/8"	3-1/8"	3-7/8"
B	4		2"	2-3/4"	3-1/2"
B	2	◺	2-3/8"	3-1/8"	6-7/8"

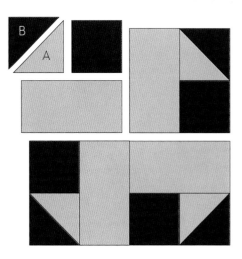

HST—pages 12-13

Seesaw Block

Color/Cut		Subcut	6"	9"	12"
*A	4 ▢		2"	2-3/4"	3-1/2"
*B	4 ▭		2" x 3-1/2"	2-3/4" x 5"	3-1/2" x 6-1/2"
*C	4 ▭		2" x 3-1/2"	2-3/4" x 5"	3-1/2" x 6-1/2"
*D	8 ▪		2"	2-3/4"	3-1/2"

*Use B rectangles and D squares to make Flying Geese from Squares, page 17. For Adding Corners, page 24, use A squares and C rectangles.

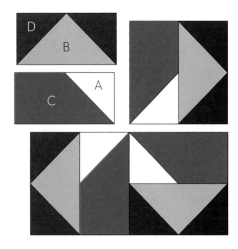

Flying Geese from Squares—page 17
Adding Corners—page 24

Shipping Dreams

Color/Cut		Subcut	6"	9"	12"
A	3 ▨	◺	2-3/8"	3-1/8"	3-7/8"
A	2 ▭		2" x 3-1/2"	2-3/4" x 5"	3-1/2" x 6-1/2"
B	1 ▭		2" x 6-1/2"	2-3/4" x 9-1/2"	3-1/2" x 12-1/2"
C	3 ▪	◺	2-3/8"	3-1/8"	3-7/8"
C	2 ▪		2"	2-3/4"	3-1/2"

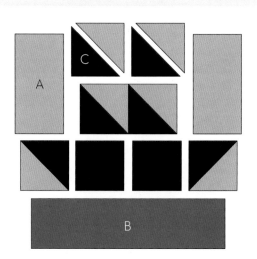

HST—pages 12-13

Shooting Star

Color/Cut		Subcut	6"	9"	12"
A	4 ▢		2"	2-3/4"	3-1/2"
A	2 ▢	◺	2-3/8"	3-1/8"	3-7/8"
B	2 ▢	◺	2-3/8"	3-1/8"	3-7/8"
C	4 ▢	◺	2-3/8"	3-1/8"	3-7/8"
D	4 ▢		2"	2-3/4"	3-1/2"

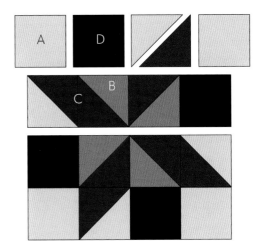

HST—pages 12-13

Single Sawtooth

Color/Cut		Subcut	6"	9"	12"
A	4 ▢		2"	2-3/4"	3-1/2"
B	4 ▢	◺	2-3/8"	3-1/8"	3-7/8"
B	4 ▢		2"	2-3/4"	3-1/2"
C	4 ▢	◺	2-3/8"	3-1/8"	3-7/8"

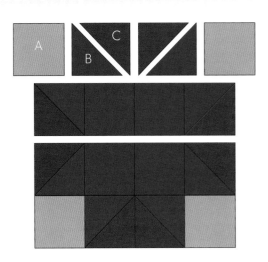

HST—pages 12-13

Single Star

Color/Cut		Subcut	6"	9"	12"
A	4		2"	2-3/4"	3-1/2"
A	4	◻	2-3/8"	3-1/8"	3-7/8"
B	4		2"	2-3/4"	3-1/2"
B	4	◻	2-3/8"	3-1/8"	3-7/8"

HST—pages 12-13

Snowflake Block

Color/Cut		Subcut	6"	9"	12"
A	7	◻	2-3/8"	3-1/8"	3-7/8"
A	2		2"	2-3/4"	3-1/2"
B	7	◻	2-3/8"	3-1/8"	3-7/8"

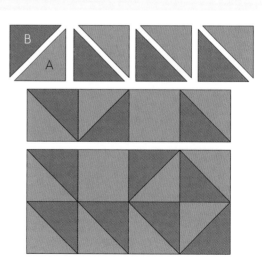

HST—pages 12-13

Solitaire Block

Color/Cut		Subcut	6"	9"	12"
A	2	⊠	2-3/4"	3-1/2"	4-1/4"
A	4	◺	2-3/8"	3-1/8"	3-7/8"
B	4	◺	2-3/8"	3-1/8"	3-7/8"
C	2	⊠	2-3/4"	3-1/2"	4-1/4"
C	2	◺	2-3/8"	3-1/8"	3-7/8"

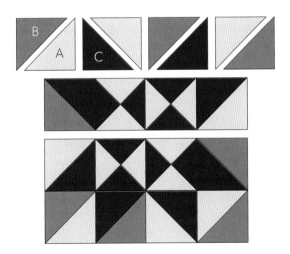

HST—pages 12-13
QST—pages 14-15

Squire Smith's Choice

Color/Cut		Subcut	6"	9"	12"
A	8	◺	2-3/8"	3-1/8"	3-7/8"
B	6	◺	2-3/8"	3-1/8"	3-7/8"
C	2	◺	2-3/8"	3-1/8"	3-7/8"

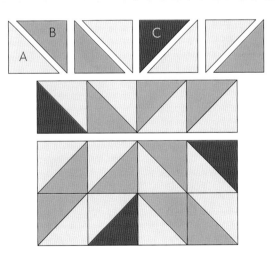

HST—pages 12-13

Star and Pinwheels

Color/Cut		Subcut	6"	9"	12"
A	6	◻️ ◿	2-3/8"	3-1/8"	3-7/8"
A	1	◻️ ⊠	2-3/4"	3-1/2"	4-1/4"
B	1	◼️ ⊠	2-3/4"	3-1/2"	4-1/4"
C	8	◼️ ◿	2-3/8"	3-1/8"	3-7/8"

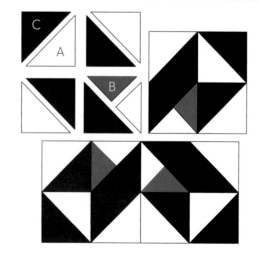

HST—pages 12-13
QST—page 14 (steps 1-4)

Star of Friendship

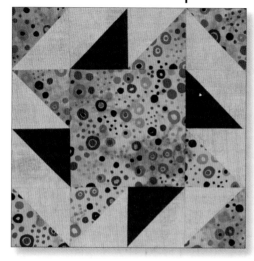

Color/Cut		Subcut	6"	9"	12"
A	6	◻️ ◺	2-3/8"	3-1/8"	3-7/8"
B	1	◻️	3-1/2"	5"	6-1/2"
B	4	◻️ ◺	2-3/8"	3-1/8"	3-7/8"
C	2	◼️ ◺	2-3/8"	3-1/8"	3-7/8"

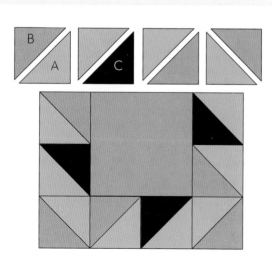

HST—pages 12-13

Star of the
Milky Way

Color/Cut		Subcut	6"	9"	12"
A	8	◺	2-3/8"	3-1/8"	3-7/8"
B	8	◹	2-3/8"	3-1/8"	3-7/8"

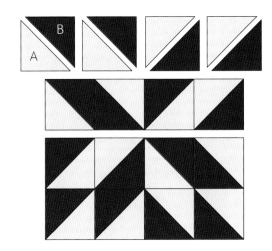

HST—pages 12-13

Star Puzzle
Block

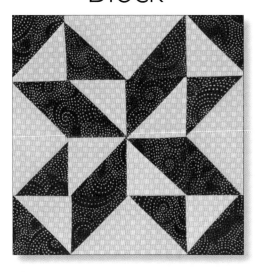

Color/Cut		Subcut	6"	9"	12"
*A	1	⊠	4-1/4"	5-3/4"	7-1/4"
A	4	◺	2-3/8"	3-1/8"	3-7/8"
*B	8	◺	2-3/8"	3-1/8"	3-7/8"

*Use A-QST for "geese" bodies and 8-B HSTs for "sky" to make Flying Geese from Triangles, page 16.

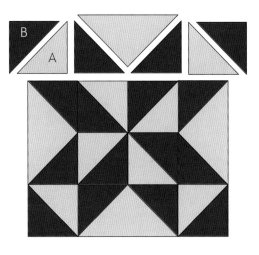

HST—pages 12-13
Flying Geese From Triangles —page 16

State of Louisiana

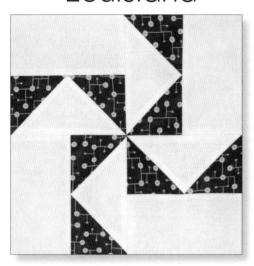

Color/Cut		Subcut	6"	9"	12"
A	4 ▭		2" x 3-1/2"	2-3/4" x 5"	3-1/2" x 6-1/2"
*A	1 ▢	⊠	4-1/4"	5-3/4"	7-1/4"
*B	4 ■	◩	2-3/8"	3-1/8"	3-7/8"

*Use A-QST for "geese" bodies and B-HSTs for "sky" to make
Flying Geese from Triangles page 16.

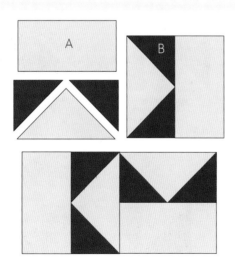

HST—pages 12-13
Flying Geese from Triangles—page 16

Sugar Bowl Block

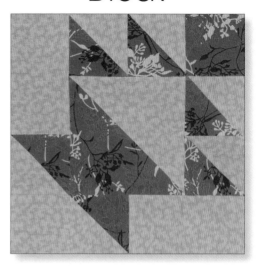

Color/Cut		Subcut	6"	9"	12"
A	1 ▨	◸	3-7/8"	5-3/8"	6-7/8"
A	2 ▭		2" x 3-1/2"	2-3/4" x 5"	3-1/2" x 6-1/2"
A	1 ▨		2"	2-3/4"	3-1/2"
A	3 ▨	◸	2-3/8"	3-1/8"	3-7/8"
B	1 ▨	◸	3-7/8"	5-3/8"	6-7/8"
B	1 ▨		2"	2-3/4"	3-1/2"
B	3 ▨	◸	2-3/8"	3-1/8"	3-7/8"

There will be triangles left over from B HST subcuts.

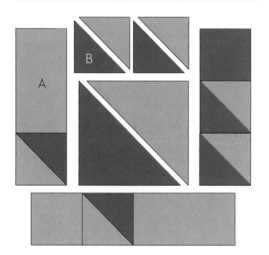

HST—pages 12-13

The Anvil

Color/Cut		Subcut	6"	9"	12"
A	4		2"	2-3/4"	3-1/2"
A	4	◻	2-3/8"	3-1/8"	3-7/8"
B	4	◻	2-3/8"	3-1/8"	3-7/8"
C	1		3-1/2"	5"	6-1/2"

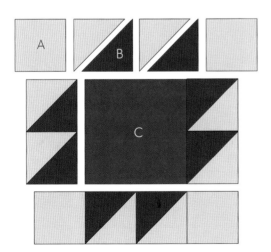

HST—pages 12-13

The Disk

Color/Cut		Subcut	6"	9"	12"
A	1	◻	3-7/8"	5-3/8"	6-7/8"
*A	2		2"	2-3/4"	3-1/2"
B	1		2"	2-3/4"	3-1/2"
*B	2		2" x 3-1/2"	2-3/4" x 5"	3-1/2" x 6-1/2"
B	1	◻	2-3/8"	3-1/8"	3-7/8"
C	1	◻	3-7/8"	5-3/8"	6-7/8"
C	2		2" x 3-1/2"	2-3/4" x 5"	3-1/2" x 6-1/2"
*C	3		2"	2-3/4"	3-1/2"
C	1	◻	2-3/8"	3-1/8"	3-7/8"

*B rectangles, 2-A and 2-C squares for Parallel Seams, page 22.

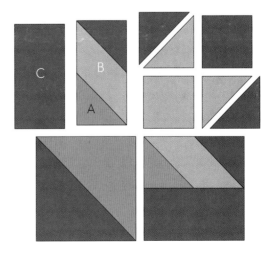

HST—pages 12-13
Parallel Seams—page 22

The Disk Variation

Color/Cut		Subcut	6"	9"	12"
A	6 ⬜		2"	2-3/4"	3-1/2"
A	3 ⬜	◻◹	2-3/8"	3-1/8"	3-7/8"
B	2 🟦	◻◹	2-3/8"	3-1/8"	3-7/8"
C	1 🟦	◻◹	2-3/8"	3-1/8"	3-7/8"
D	1 ◼	◻◹	3-7/8"	5-3/8"	6-7/8"
E	1 ⬛	◻◹	2-3/8"	3-1/8"	3-7/8"
E	1 ⬛	◻◹	2"	2-3/4"	3-1/2"

There will be a triangle left over from D HST subcut.

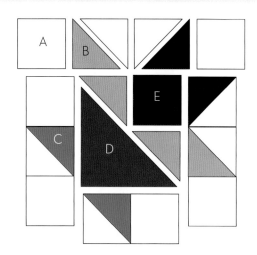

HST—pages 12-13
Adding Triangles to a Square—page 23

Triangle Squares

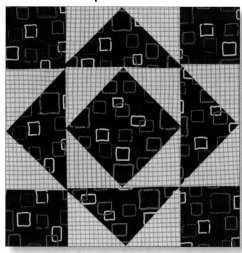

Color/Cut		Subcut	6"	9"	12"
A	4 🟦		2"	2-3/4"	3-1/2"
*A	4 🟦		2-3/8"	3-1/8"	3-7/8"
B	1 ◼		3-1/2"	5"	6-1/2"
*B	1 ◼		4-1/4"	5-3/4"	7-1/2"
C	4 ◼		2"	2-3/4"	3-1/2"

*Use 4-A squares and the large B square to make Four-at-a-Time Flying Geese, page 18.

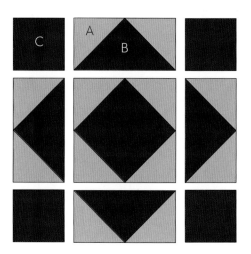

Square-in-a-Square—page 23
Four-at-a-time Flying Geese—page 18

Triangle Weave

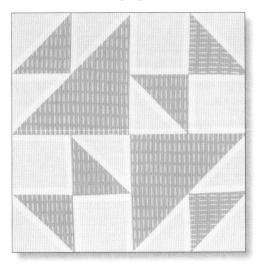

Color/Cut		Subcut	6"	9"	12"
A	4		2"	2-3/4"	3-1/2"
A	5		2-3/8"	3-1/8"	3-7/8"
B	1		3-7/8"	5-3/8"	6-7/8"
B	3		2-3/8"	3-1/8"	3-7/8"

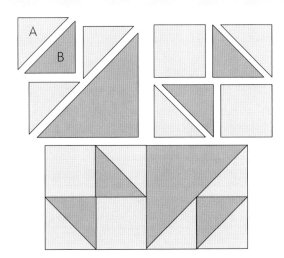

HST—pages 12-13
Adding Triangles to a Square—page 25

Twelve Triangles

Color/Cut		Subcut	6"	9"	12"
A	1		3-1/2"	5"	6-1/2"
B	8		2"	2-3/4"	3-1/2"
*B	4		2-3/8"	3-1/8"	3-7/8"
*C	1		4-1/4"	5-3/4"	7-1/4"

*Use 4-B squares and the C square to make Four-at-a-Time Flying Geese, page 18.

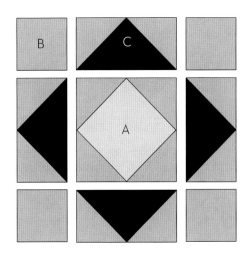

Square-in-a-Square—page 23
Four-at-a-Time Flying Geese—page 18

Virginia Reel

Color/Cut		Subcut	6"	9"	12"
*A	1		4-1/4"	5-3/4"	7-1/4"
*A	4		2-3/8"	3-1/8"	3-7/8"
*B	1		4-1/4"	5-3/4"	7-1/4"
*B	4		2-3/8"	3-1/8"	3-7/8"

*Use large A square/small B squares, and large B square/small A squares to make Four-at-a-Time Flying Geese, page 18.

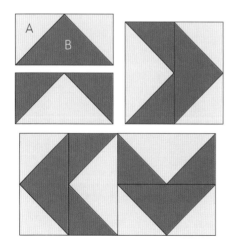

Four-at-a-time Flying Geese—page 18

Waypoint Star

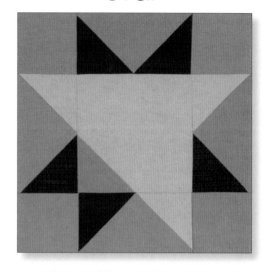

Color/Cut		Subcut	6"	9"	12"
*A	1		3-1/2"	5"	6-1/2"
*A	3		2"	2-3/4"	3-1/2"
*B	5		2"	2-3/4"	3-1/2"
*B	4		2" x 3-1/2"	2-3/4" x 5"	3-1/2" x 6-1/2"
*C	5		2"	2-3/4"	3-1/2"

*Use 3-A squares, 5-C squares, and 4-B rectangles to make Flying Geese from Squares, page 17, and large A square and 1-B square for Adding Corners, page 24.

Block designed by Sue Voegtlin

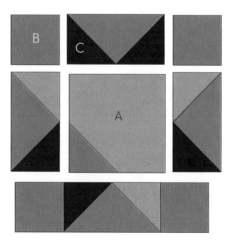

Flying Geese from Squares—page 17
Adding Corners—page 24

Whirligig

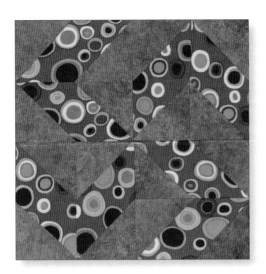

Color/Cut		Subcut	6"	9"	12"
A	16		2"	2-3/4"	3-1/2"
B	8		2" x 3-1/2"	2-3/4 x 5"	3-1/2" x 6-1/2"

Virginia Reel, page 110, and Whirligig are similar. One is made with flying geese and the other with parallel seams.

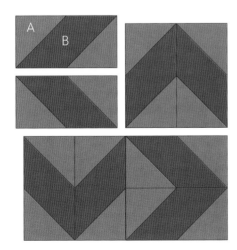

Parallel Seams—page 22

Whirlpool Block

Color/Cut		Subcut	6"	9"	12"
*A	12		2"	2-3/4"	3-1/2"
A	2	◻	2-3/8"	3-1/8"	3-7/8"
B	1		3-1/2"	5"	6-1/2"
*B	4		2" x 3-1/2"	2-3/4" x 5"	3-1/2" x 6-1/2"
B	2	◻	2-3/8"	3-1/8"	3-7/8"

*Use 8-A squares and 4-B rectangles to make Flying Geese from Squares, page 17.

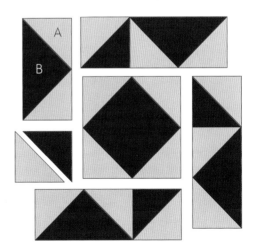

HST—pages 12-13
Flying Geese from Squares—page 17
Square-in-a-Square—page 23
Partial Seams—page 20

Wild Duck

Color/Cut		Subcut	6"	9"	12"
A	4		2"	2-3/4"	3-1/2"
A	3	◻	2-3/8"	3-1/8"	3-7/8"
B	4		2"	2-3/4"	3-1/2"
C	4	◻	2-3/8"	3-1/8"	3-7/8"

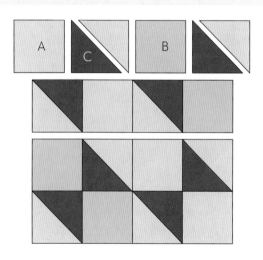

HST—pages 12-13

Windblown Square

Color/Cut		Subcut	6"	9"	12"
A	1		3-1/2"	5"	6-1/2"
*A	8		2"	2-3/4"	3-1/2"
A	2	◻	2-3/8"	3-1/8"	3-7/8"
B	2		2"	2-3/4"	3-1/2"
B	1	◻	2-3/8"	3-1/8"	3-7/8"
*B	2		2 x 3-1/2"	2-3/4" x 5"	3-1/2" x 6-1/2"
*C	2		2 x 3-1/2"	2-3/4" x 5"	3-1/2" x 6-1/2"
C	2		2"	2-3/4"	3-1/2"
C	1	◻	2-3/8"	3-1/8"	3-7/8"

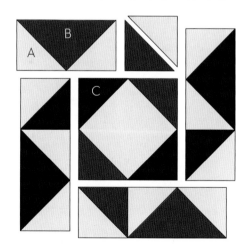

*Flying Geese from Squares page 17
HST—pages 12-13; Partial Seams—page 20
Square-in-a-Square—page 23

Windmill Block

Color/Cut		Subcut	6"	9"	12"
A	4		2-3/8"	3-1/8"	3-7/8"
B	2		2-3/8"	3-1/8"	3-7/8"
B	1		4-1/4"	5-3/4"	7-1/4"
C	2		2-3/8"	3-1/8"	3-7/8"
D	1		4-1/4"	5-3/4"	7-1/4"

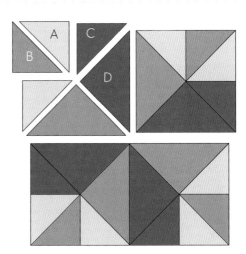

HST—pages 12-13
QST—page 14 (steps 1-4)
Adding Triangles to a Square—page 25

Windmill Block Variation

Color/Cut		Subcut	6"	9"	12"
A	4		2"	2-3/4"	3-1/2"
*A	1		4-1/4"	5-3/4"	7-1/2"
*B	4		2-3/8"	3-1/8"	3-7/8"
B	4		2"	2-3/4"	3-1/2"

*Use 4-B squares and 1-A square to make Four-at-a-Time Flying Geese, page 18.

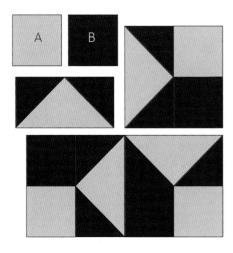

Four-at-a-Time Flying Geese—page 18

113

Yankee Puzzle

Color/Cut		Subcut	6"	9"	12"
A	1		4-1/4"	5-3/4	7-1/4"
*A	8		2-3/8"	3-1/8"	3-7/8"
*B	1		4-1/4"	5-3/4"	7-1/4"
B	2	◻	2-3/8"	3-1/8"	3-7/8"
C	2	◻	4-1/4"	5-3/4"	7-1/4"

*Use 8-A squares and 1-B square to make Four-at-a-Time Flying Geese on page 18.

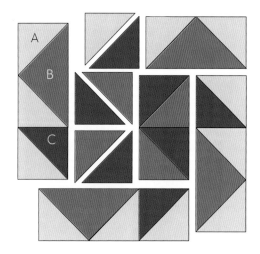

HST—pages 12-13
Four-at-a-Time Flying Geese—page 18
Partial Seams—page 20

Wondering What To Do With Your Blocks?

Whether you made a lot of the same block or you made a variety, here are some ways to play around with them.

1. Organize a block swap with some quilting friends and, as a group, choose the number of blocks to exchange based on a finished project idea. Everyone makes the block design they choose. If you want the finished quilt to be coordinated, as a group, choose a colorway or a fabric collection to use. When everyone is finished making their blocks, swap away!

2. Create a Block Library. I used three ring scrapbooking binders with plastic sleeves to store my blocks. They are organized by grid size, alphabetized, and original instructions are tucked behind each block. Since the blocks have raw edges, it's a gentler way to store them without fraying.

3. Practice your quilting. I really like utility stitching. I chose a few blocks and used them to practice some utility and embroidery stitches. I made my blocks 9-inches so they are a reasonable size to handle when I stitch by hand.

4. Take a photo of a block and play around with placement and color on your computer or an app on your smart phone. Since I'm a photographer I use Photoshop. On the following page are some examples of how I manipulated blocks to make a secondary pattern. You can flip, rotate or create a mirror image. Using technology to "test" block designs is a quick, fun way to experiment and it's exciting see what happens in the process!

5. Make a quilt using one of the settings on pages 133-141. Remember that sashing helps set blocks apart from one another, making the block designs stand out. Pay attention to grid sizes if you choose not to add sashing. Blocks evenly divisible by 2 and 4 sit well together. Blocks divisible by 3 do the same. In both cases, seam lines will either line up or divide a section equally which is more pleasing to the eye.

Louisiana Pinwheel
Page 37

Aunt Dinah
Page 117

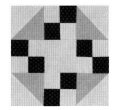

Prairie Queen
Page 127

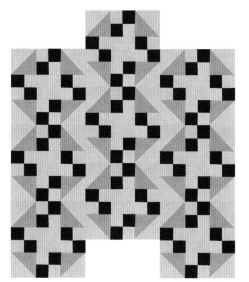

Magnolia Block
Page 124

The 6 x 6 Grid Blocks

When it came time to make 6 x 6 grid blocks, I was a bit apprehensive. The pieces were smaller and the number of parts within the block increased dramatically. But I loved the detail that started to appear as more pieces were added to the block. Since the pieces were smaller, it was a great way to use up my little scraps that seemed too small to save. It turns out, these blocks became my favorite to make.

Aunt Dinah

Color/Cut		Subcut	6"	9"	12"
A	2		2-7/8"	3-7/8"	4-7/8"
A	4		1-7/8"	2-3/8"	2-7/8"
A	1		3-1/4"	4-1/4"	5-1/4"
A	1		2-1/2"	3-1/2"	4-1/2"
B	1		3-1/4"	4-1/4"	5-1/4"
B	4		1-1/2"	2"	2-1/2"
B	2		2-7/8"	3-7/8"	4-7/8"

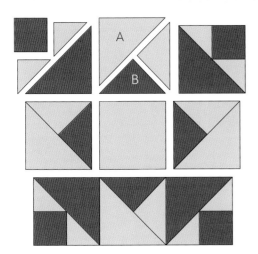

HST—pages 12-13
QST—page 14 (steps 1-4)
Adding Triangles to a Squrте—page 25

Aunt Sukey's Choice

Color/Cut		Subcut	6"	9"	12"
*A	12		1-1/2"	2"	2-1/2"
*A	8		1-1/2" x 2-1/2"	2" x 3-1/2"	2-1/2" x 4-1/2"
*B	12		1-1/2"	2"	2-1/2"
*B	4		1-1/2" x 2-1/2"	2" x 3-1/2"	2-1/2" x 4-1/2"
C	1		2-1/2"	3-1/2"	4-1/2"

*Use 8-A squares/4-B rectangles and 8-B squares/4-A rectangles to make Flying Geese from Squares on page 17.

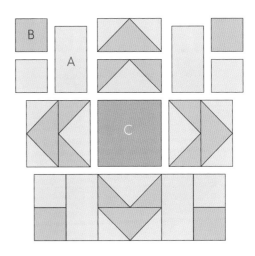

Flying Geese from Squares—page 17

117

Bowl of Fruit

Color/Cut	Subcut	6"	9"	12"
A 2 ⬜		2-1/2"	3-1/2"	4-1/2"
A 1 ⬜	◺	2-7/8"	3-7/8"	4-7/8"
B 1 ⬛		1-1/2"	2"	2-1/2"
B 1 ⬛	◺	2-7/8"	3-7/8"	4-7/8"
C 21 ⬛		1-1/2"	2"	2-1/2"
assorted colors				

There will be triangles left over from A & B HST subcuts.

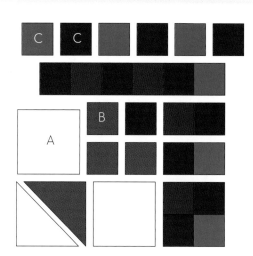

HST—pages 12-13

Building Blocks

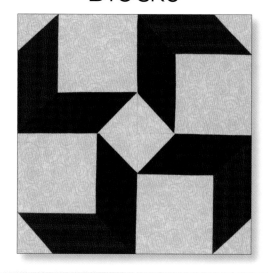

Color/Cut	Subcut	6"	9"	12"
A 4		2-1/2"	3-1/2"	4-1/2"
*A 8		1-1/2"	2"	2-1/2"
*B 4		1-1/2" x 3-1/2"	2" x 5"	2-1/2" x 6-1/2"
*C 4		1-1/2"	2"	2-1/2"
*C 4		1-1/2" x 2-1/2"	2" x 3-1/2"	2-1/2" x 4-1/2"

*Use 4-B rectangles, 4-A, 4-C squares, to make Parallel Seams on page 22. For Adding Corners on page 24, Use 4-C rectangles and 4-A squares.

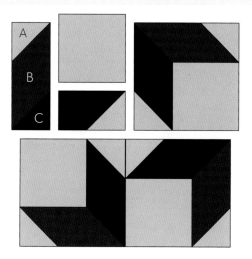

Adding Corners—page 24
Parallel Seams—page 22

Children's Delight

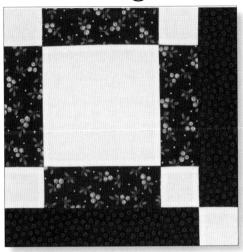

Color/Cut		Subcut	6"	9"	12"
A	1		3-1/2"	5"	6-1/2"
A	5		1-1/2"	2"	2-1/2"
B	4		1-1/2" x 3-1/2"	2" x 5"	2-1/2" x 6-1/2"
C	2		1-1/2" x 5-1/2""	2" x 8-1/2""	2-1/2" x 11-1/2""

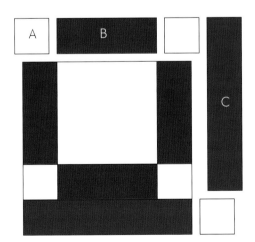

You can try switching out the darks and lights in this block for a different look.

Crossword Block

Color/Cut		Subcut	6"	9"	12"
A	8		1-1/2" x 2-1/2"	2" x 3-1/2"	2-1/2" x 4-1/2"
A	10		1-1/2"	2"	2-1/2"
B	10		1-1/2"	2"	2-1/2"

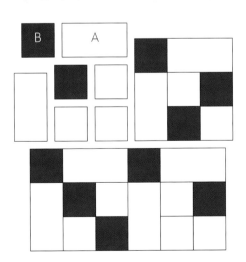

For a different look, switch out the "B" squares with other colors. Make four blocks and see what kind of secondary patterns start to appear.

Domino Block (light)

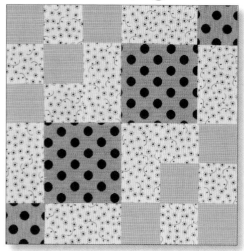

Color/Cut		Subcut	6"	9"	12"
A	6		1-1/2" x 2-1/2"	2" x 3-1/2"	2-1/2" x 4-1/2"
A	6		1-1/2"	2"	2-1/2"
B	8		1-1/2"	2"	2-1/2"
C	2		2-1/2"	3-1/2"	4-1/2"
C	2		1-1/2"	2"	2-1/2"

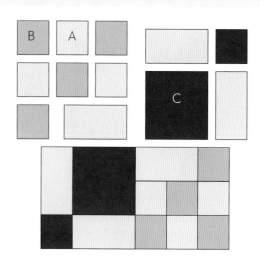

Since there are so many seams in this block, use pins to match them up.

Domino Quilt Block (dark)

Color/Cut		Subcut	6"	9"	12"
A	8		1-1/2"	2"	2-1/2"
B	2		2-1/2"	3-1/2"	4-1/2"
B	2		1-1/2"	2"	2-1/2"
C	6		1-1/2"	2"	2-1/2"
C	2		1-1/2" x 2-1/2"	2" x 3-1/2"	2-1/2" x 4-1/2"
D	4		1-1/2" x 2-1/2"	2" x 3-1/2"	2-1/2" x 4-1/2"

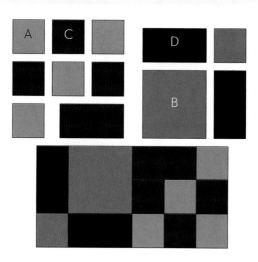

It's interesting to see how color can change the look of the Domino block, switching from lights to darks.

Flagstones Block

Color/Cut	Subcut	6"	9"	12"
A 10 ⬜		1-1/2"	2"	2-1/2"
*A 2 ⬜		3-1/2"	5"	6-1/2"
*B 16 ⬛		1-1/2"	2"	2-1/2"

*For Adding Corners, page 24, use 2 large A squares and 8-B squares.

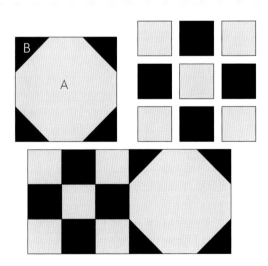

Adding Corners—page 24

Flying Darts Block

Color/Cut	Subcut	6"	9"	12"
A 4 ▭		1-1/2" x 3-1/2"	2" x 5""	2-1/2" x 6-1/2"
*A 2 ▭		1-1/2" x 2-1/2"	2" x 3-1/2""	2-1/2" x 4-1/2"
A 2 ⬜	⊠	3-1/4"	4-1/4"	5-1/4"
*A 4 ⬜		1-1/2"	2"	2-1/2"
*B 2 ▨		1-1/2" x 2-1/2"	2" x 3-1/2"	2-1/2" x 4-1/2"
B 2 ▨	⊠	3-1/4"	4-1/4"	5-1/4"
*B 4 ▨		1-1/2"	2"	2-1/2"

*Use 2-A rectangles/4-B squares, and 2-B rectangles/4-A squares to make Flying Geese from Squares on page 17.

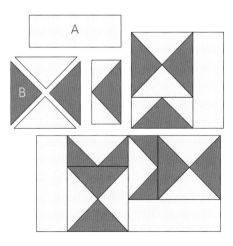

QST—page 15
Flying Geese from Squares—page 17

Four Crowns

Color/Cut		Subcut	6"	9"	12"
A	4	◻◹	1-7/8"	2-3/8""	2-7/8"
*A	8		1-1/2"	2"	2-1/2"
*A	4		1-1/2" x 2-1/2"	2" x 3-1/2"	2-1/2" x 4-1/2"
*B	4		1-1/2" x 2-1/2"	2" x 3-1/2"	2-1/2" x 4-1/2"
B	2	◻◹	2-7/8"	3-7/8"	4-7/8"
*B	8		1-1/2"	2"	2-1/2"
C	1		2-1/2"	3-1/2"	4-1/2"
C	4		1-1/2"	2"	2-1/2"

*Use 8-A squares/4-B rectangles and 8-B squares/4-A rectangles to make Flying Geese from Squares on page 17.

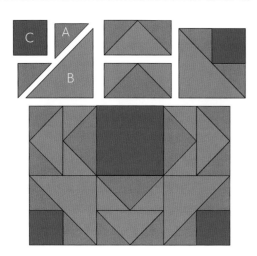

HST—pages 12-13
*Flying Geese from Squares—page 17
Adding Triangles to a Square—page 23

Framed Squares

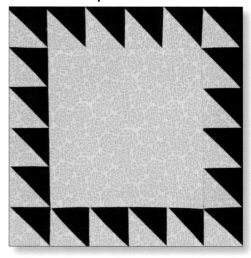

Color/Cut		Subcut	6"	9"	12"
A	1	◻		4-1/2"	6-1/2"	8-1/2"
A	10	◻◹	1-7/8"	2-3/8"	2-7/8"
B	10	◼◹	1-7/8"	2-3/8"	2-7/8"

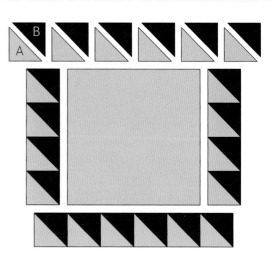

HST—pages 12-13
Pay attention to orientation of HSTs.

Hour Glass

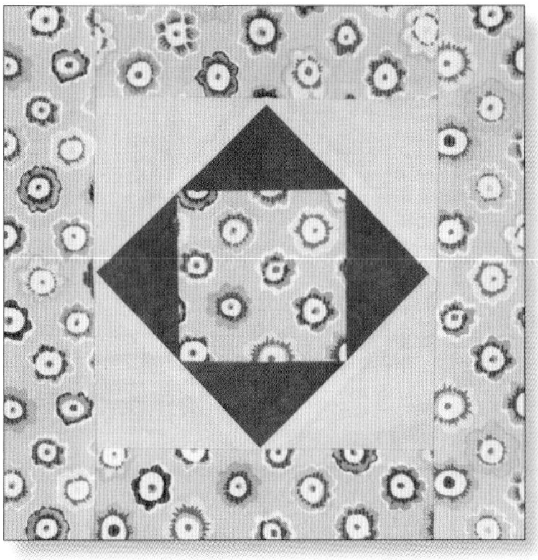

Color/Cut		Subcut	6"	9"	12"
A	4		2-1/2"	3-1/2"	4-1/2"
B	1		2-1/2"	3-1/2"	4-1/2"
B	2		1-1/2" x 4-1/2"	2" x 6-1/2"	2-1/2" x 8-1/2"
B	2		1-1/2" x 6-1/2"	2" x 9-1/2"	2-1/2" x 12-1/2"
C	4		1-1/2"	2"	2-1/2"

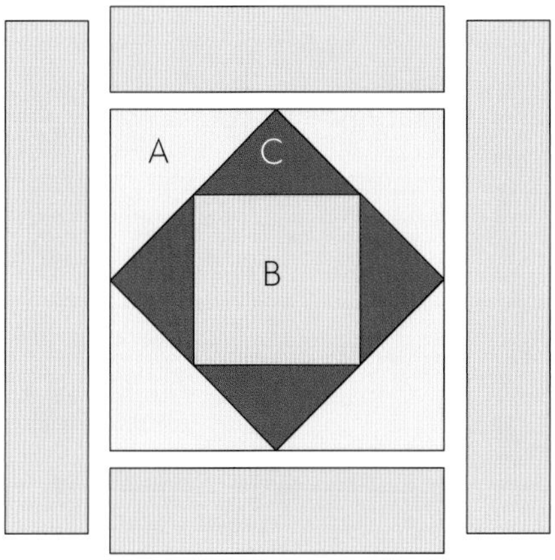

HST—pages 12-13
Square-in-a-Square—page 25

Jacob's Ladder

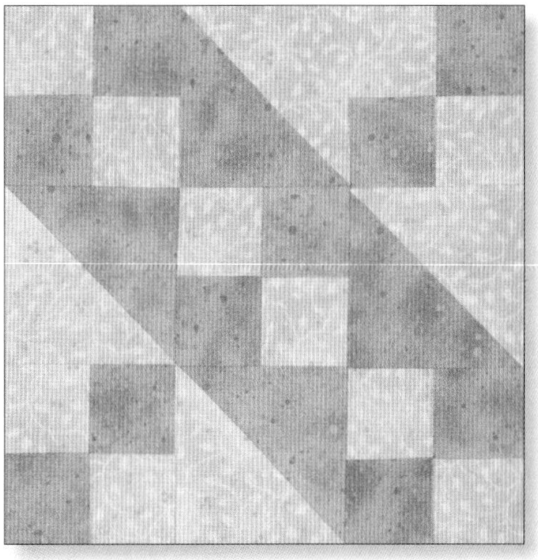

Color/Cut		Subcut	6"	9"	12"
A	2		2-7/8"	3-7/8"	4-7/8"
A	10		1-1/2"	2"	2-1/2"
B	2		2-7/8"	3-7/8"	4-7/8"
B	10		1-1/2"	2"	2-1/2"

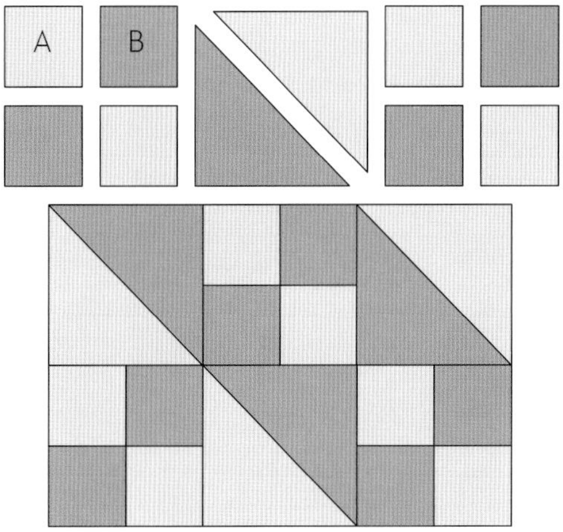

HST—pages 12-13

Lady of the Lake

Color/Cut		Subcut	6"	9"	12"
A	1		4-7/8"	6-7/8"	8-7/8"
A	10		1-7/8"	2-3/8"	2-7/8"
B	1		4-7/8"	6-7/8"	8-7/8"
B	10		1-7/8"	2-3/8"	2-7/8"

There will be triangles left over from A and B HST subcuts.

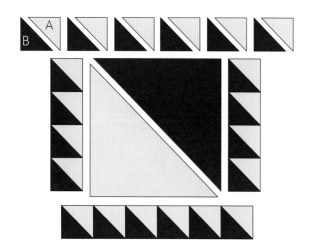

HST—pages 12-13

Magnolia Block

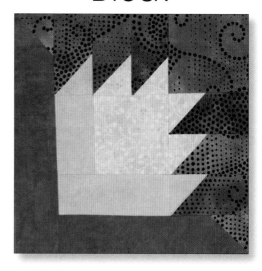

Color/Cut		Subcut	6"	9"	12"
A	1		2-1/2"	3-1/2"	4-1/2"
*A	4		1-1/2"	2"	2-1/2"
*B	2		1-1/2"	2"	2-1/2"
B	1		1-1/2" x 2-1/2"	2" x 3-1/2"	2-1/2" x 4-1/2"
B	1		1-1/2" x 3-1/2"	2" x 5"	2-1/2" x 6-1/2"
*C	6		1-1/2" x 2-1/2"	2" x 3-1/2"	2-1/2" x 4-1/2"
C	1		2-1/2"	3-1/2"	4-1/2"
*C	2		1-1/2"	2"	2-1/2"
*D	1		1-1/2" x 5-1/2"	2" x 8"	2-1/2" x 10-1/2"
*D	1		1-1/2" x 6-1/2"	2" x 9-1/2"	2-1/2" x 12-1/2"

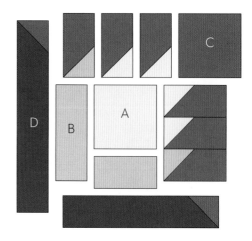

*For Adding Corners on page 24, use squares and rectangles.

Maple Leaf Block

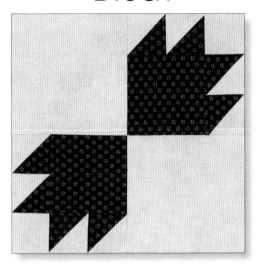

Color/Cut		Subcut	6"	9"	12"
A	2		3-1/2"	5"	6-1/2"
A	4	◺	1-7/8"	2-3/8"	2-7/8"
A	2		1-1/2"	2"	2-1/2"
B	2		2-1/2"	3-1/2"	4-1/2"
B	4	◺	1-7/8"	2-3/8"	2-7/8"

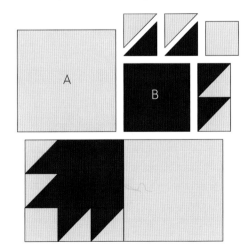

HST—pages 12-13

Maple Leaf Variation

Color/Cut		Subcut	6"	9"	12"
A	4		1-1/2" x 2-1/2"	2" x 3-1/2"	2-1/2" x 4-1/2"
B	1		2-1/2"	3-1/2"	4-1/2"
*B	12		1-1/2"	2"	2-1/2"
*C	8		1-1/2" x 2-1/2"	2" x 3-1/2"	2-1/2" x 4-1/2"
C	4		1-1/2"	2"	2-1/2"

*Use 8-B squares and 4-C rectangles to make Flying Geese from Squares on page 17.

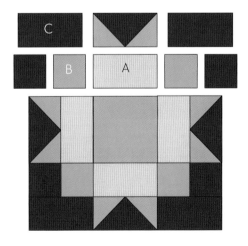

Flying Geese from Squares—page 17

Old Crow

Color/Cut		Subcut	6"	9"	12"
A	2 ☐		2-1/2"	3-1/2"	4-1/2"
A	8 ☐	◺	1-7/8"	2-3/8"	2-7/8"
A	2 ☐		1-1/2"	2"	2-1/2"
B	2 ■		2-1/2"	3-1/2"	4-1/2"
B	8 ■	◺	1-7/8"	2-3/8"	2-7/8"
B	2 ■		1-1/2"	2"	2-1/2"

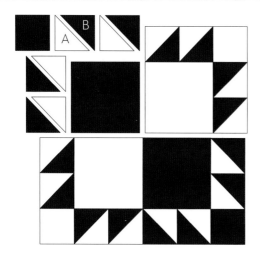

HST—pages 12-13
Pay attention orientation of HSTs.

Ozark Maple Leaf

Color/Cut		Subcut	6"	9"	12"
A	2 ▨		2-1/2"	3-1/2"	4-1/2"
A	4 ▨		1-1/2"	2"	2-1/2"
A	4 ▨	◺	1-7/8"	2-3/8"	2-7/8"
B	6 ■		1-1/2"	2"	2-1/2"
B	4 ■	◺	1-7/8"	2-3/8"	2-7/8"
B	2 ▬		1-1/2" x 2-1/2"	2" x 3-1/2"	2-1/2" x 4-1/2"
B	2 ▬		1-1/2" x 3-1/2"	2" x 5"	2-1/2" x 6-1/2"

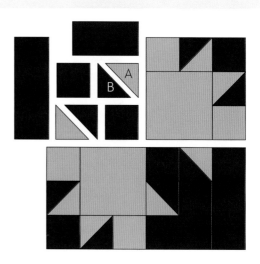

HST—pages 12-13

Prairie Queen

Color/Cut		Subcut	6"	9"	12"
A	2	◻	2-7/8"	3-7/8"	4-7/8"
A	8		1-1/2"	2"	2-1/2"
A	1		2-1/2"	3-1/2"	4-1/2"
B	2	◻	2-7/8"	3-7/8"	4-7/8"
C	8		1-1/2"	2"	2-1/2"

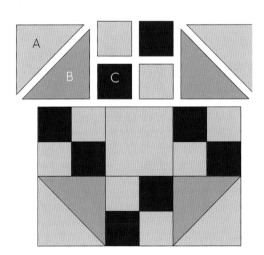

HST—pages 12-13

Pudding and Pie

Color/Cut		Subcut	6"	9"	12"
A	4		1-1/2" x 3-1/2"	2" x 5"	2-1/2" x 6-1/2"
*A	8		1-1/2"	2"	2-1/2"
B	4		1-1/2" x 3-1/2"	2" x 5"	2-1/2" x 6-1/2"
*C	4		1-1/2" x 2-1/2"	2" x 3-1/2"	2-1/2" x 4-1/2"

*For Adding Corners, use 4-A squares and C rectangles.

The four segments of this block are identical; they are simply turned to make the pattern.

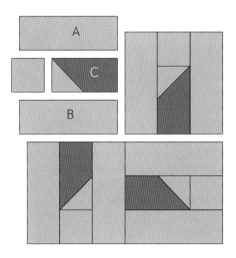

Adding Corners—page 24

Quatrefoil Block

Color/Cut	Subcut	6"	9"	12"
A 1 ☐		2-1/2"	3-1/2"	4-1/2"
*A 16 ☐		1-1/2"	2"	2-1/2"
B 4 ▨		1-1/2"	2"	2-1/2"
*C 4 ◼		2-1/2"	3-1/2"	4-1/2"
C 4 ◼		1-1/2"	2"	2-1/2"

*For Adding Corners, page 24, use B, C, & D squares.

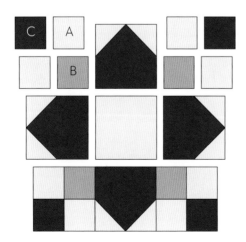

Adding Corners—page 24

Queen's Favorite

Color/Cut	Subcut	6"	9"	12"
A 1 ▨		2-1/2"	3-1/2"	4-1/2"
*B 20 ▨		1-1/2"	2"	2-1/2"
*C 8 ▨		2-1/2"	3-1/2"	4-1/2"
*D 16 ◼		1-1/2"	2"	2-1/2"

*For Adding Corners, page 24, use B, C, & D squares.

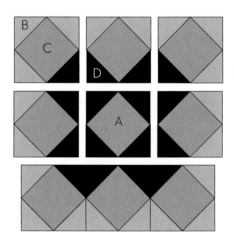

Square-in-a-Square—page 23
Adding Corners—page 24

Red Cross

Color/Cut	Subcut	6"	9"	12"
A 2		3-1/2"	5"	6-1/2"
A 8		1-1/2"	2"	2-1/2"
B 2		1-1/2" x 3-1/2"	2" x 5"	2-1/2" x 6-1/2"
B 4		1-1/2"	2"	2-1/2"

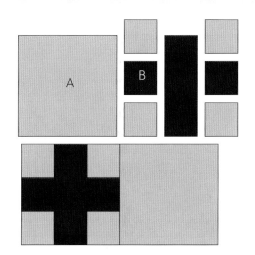

Summer Winds

Color/Cut	Subcut	6"	9"	12"
A 4		1-1/2" x 2-1/2"	2" x 3-1/2"	2-1/2" x 4-1/2"
A 10	◻	1-7/8"	2-3/8"	2-7/8"
B 2	◻	2-7/8"	3-7/8"	4-7/8"
B 6	◻	1-7/8"	2-3/8"	2-7/8"
B 4		1-1/2"	2"	2-1/2"

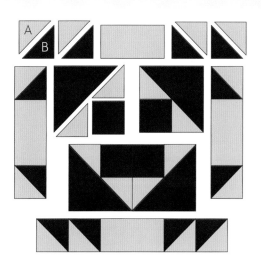

HST—pages 12-13
Adding Triangles to a Square —page 25

True Blue Quilt Block

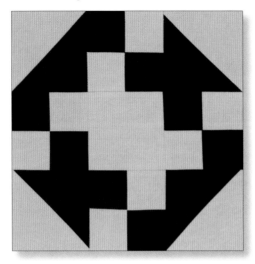

Color/Cut		Subcut	6"	9"	12"
A	2	◸	2-7/8"	3-7/8"	4-7/8"
A	1		2-1/2"	3-1/2"	4-1/2"
A	8		1-1/2"	2"	2-1/2"
B	2	◸	2-7/8"	3-7/8"	4-7/8"
B	8		1-1/2"	2"	2-1/2"

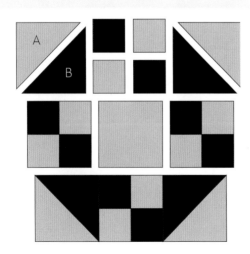

HST—pages 12-13

Wagon Tracks

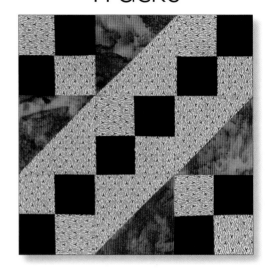

Color/Cut		Subcut	6"	9"	12"
A	10		1-1/2"	2"	2-1/2"
A	2	◸	2-7/8"	3-7/8"	4-7/8"
B	2	◸	2-7/8"	3-7/8"	4-7/8"
C	10		1-1/2"	2"	2-1/2"

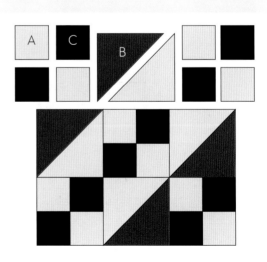

HST—pages 12-13

Wampum Block

Color/Cut	Subcut	6"	9"	12"
A 9 ☐ ◺		1-7/8"	2-3/8"	2-7/8"
B 3 ☐ ◺		1-7/8"	2-3/8"	2-7/8"
C 1 ▬		2-1/2" x 6-1/2"	3-1/2" x 9-1/2"	4-1/2" x 12-1/2"
C 3 ☐ ◺		2-7/8"	3-7/8"	4-7/8"

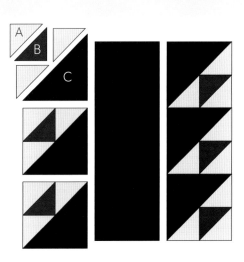

HST—pages 12-13
Adding Triangles to a Square—page 25

Weathervane Block

Color/Cut	Subcut	6"	9"	12"
*A 12 ☐		1-1/2"	2"	2-1/2"
A 4 ☐ ◺		1-7/8"	2-3/8"	2-7/8"
B 1 ☐		2-1/2"	3-1/2"	4-1/2"
B 4 ☐		1-1/2"	2"	2-1/2"
B 4 ☐ ◺		1-7/8"	2-3/8"	2-7/8"
*C 4 ☐		2-1/2"	3-1/2"	4-1/2"

For Adding Corners on page 24, use 8-A squares and 4-C squares.

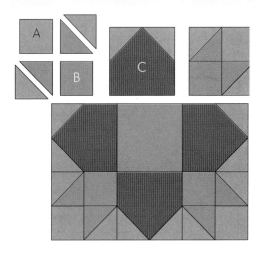

HST—pages 12-13
Adding Corners—page 24

Whirling Pinwheel

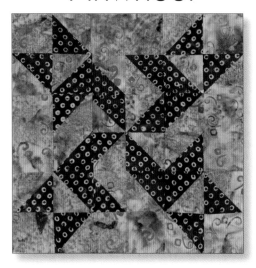

Color/Cut		Subcut	6"	9"	12"
A	4		1-1/2"	2"	2-1/2"
A	12	◻	1-7/8"	2-3/8"	2-7/8"
A	4		1-1/2" x 2-1/2"	2" x 3-1/2"	2-1/2" x 4-1/2"
B	12	◻	1-7/8"	2-3/8"	2-7/8"

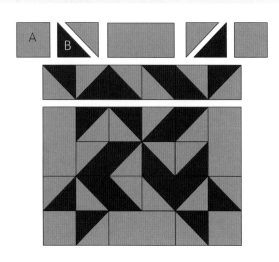

HST—pages 12-13

Windblown Block

Color/Cut		Subcut	6"	9"	12"
A	2	◻	1-1/2"	2"	2-1/2"
A	2	▭	1-1/2" x 3-1/2"	2" x 5"	2-1/2" x 6-1/2"
A	2	▭	1-1/2" x 4-1/2"	2" x 6-1/2"	2-1/2" x 8-1/2"
B	4	◻	1-1/2"	2"	2-1/2"
C	8	◻	1-1/2"	2"	2-1/2"
D	8	◻	1-1/2"	2"	2-1/2"

Designed by Sue Voegtlin

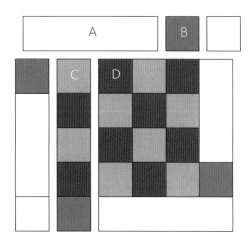

Pay attention to your quarter-inch seams to make all these little blocks fit together perfectly.

Settings & Charts

Have you made blocks and want to arrange them in a quilt setting? Here are four options to consider. You may choose to make an entire quilt but these settings could also be used for smaller projects like a lap quilt, table runner, or even a wallhanging. I included coloring pages for you to copy and experiment with your own color choices.

If you have made favorite blocks that you want to showcase in a single project, try a quilt sampler. If you made blocks from different grid sizes, it might be a good idea to separate them with sashing. Grid sizes divisible by 2 work well together because the seams and pieces will match up evenly. A 3-grid block sitting next to a 4-grid block doesn't work as well because of the difference in seam alignment. Sashing will not only set each block apart but it will downplay the differences.

STRAIGHT SETTING

The setting below includes sashing with cornerstones, however, a straight setting can also be:

- Block-to-Block

- Alternate (block and setting squares)

- Alternate block (two block designs, arranged every other one)

- Sashing (continuous sashing, sashing with cornerstones, pieced sashing)

Flock of Geese
2 x 2
Page 33

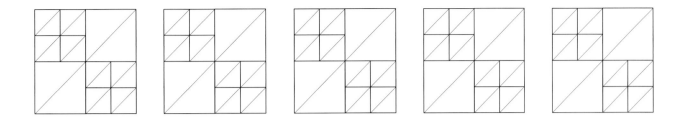

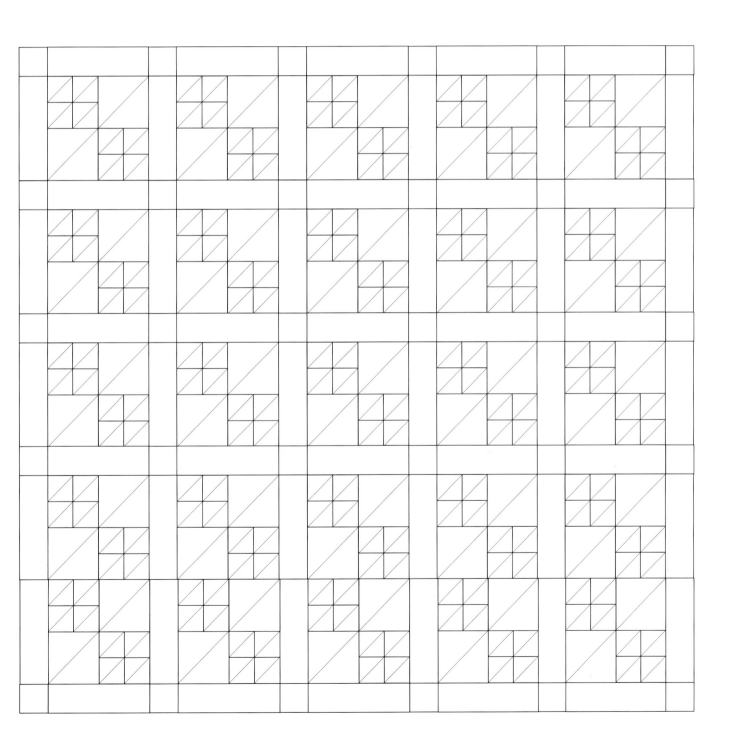

ON-POINT SETTING

An on-point, or diagonal setting simply means the blocks are set at a 45- degree angle, with side and corner setting triangles. The setting shown here is set block-to-block, creating an interesting secondary pattern where the corner squares create a four-patch. Blocks can also be set on-point using alternate blocks or with sashing.

Aunt Sukey's Choice is a block that changes drastically depending on color placement, where you place the darkest and lightest values, and how you set the blocks. Make a copy of the line drawing on page 137 and play around with value and color placement. You might design a completely new quilt!

Aunt Sukey's Choice
6 x 6
Page 117

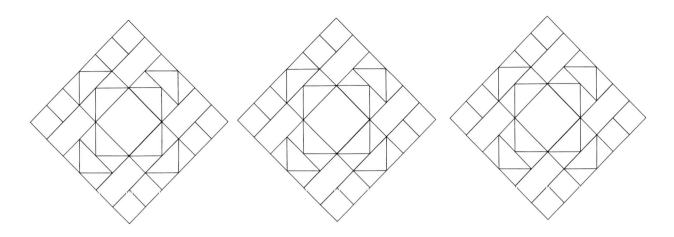

MEDALLION SETTING

A traditional medallion setting has a center focal block or design, often set on-point, with multiple (pieced and non-pieced) borders or frames added around it. The pieced borders of a medallion quilt often incorporate quilt blocks.

The setting I created is a modern, or contemporary medallion, pieced using more of the same block but varying the sashing and borders to highlight the center medallion. Notice how the Homeward Bound block is one of those blocks that can create secondary patterns and even new block designs.

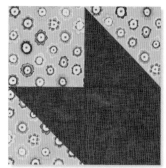

Homeward Bound
2 x 2
Page 36

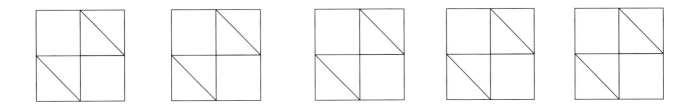

ASYMMETRICAL SETTING

Non-traditional settings have been used by makers of utility quilts for decades (i.e. Gee's Bend quilters, frontier women and housewives re-purposing clothing scraps). More recently, modern quilters have embraced the non-traditional, asymmetrical layouts with more negative space and simple design elements. These non-traditional settings may or may not incorporate quilt "blocks." The setting below is one example of how a traditional block, Patience Corners, can be colored and set in a very modern way.

Patience Corners
4 x 4
Page 97

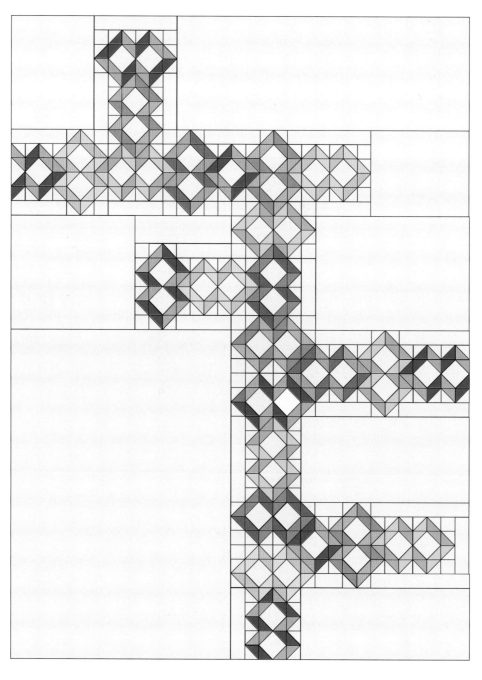

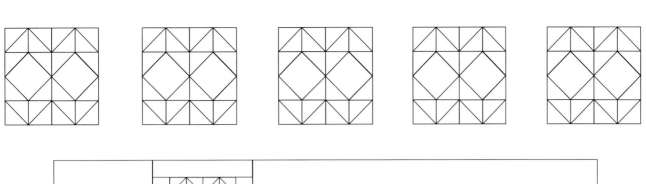

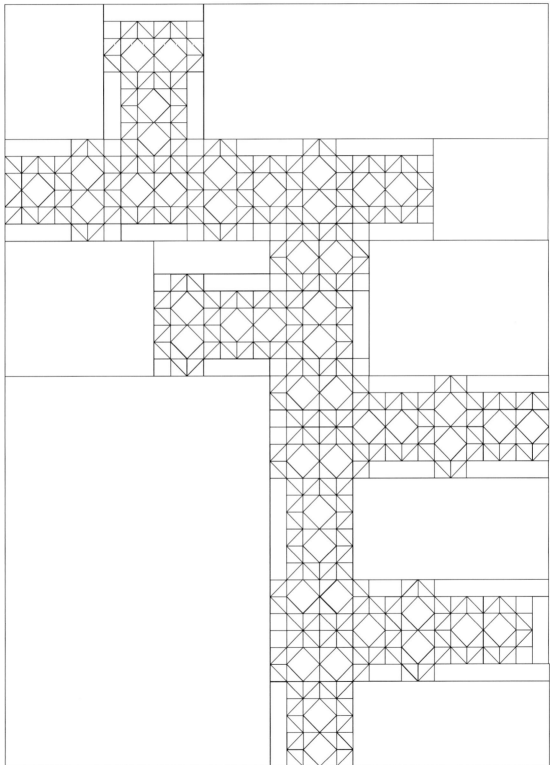

NO MATH GRID MEASUREMENTS

The measurements below were used to write instructions for blocks in this book. For each grid size I've calculated the number of squares in each grid and the finished size for each square within a 6, 9, and 12-inch finished quilt block. Based on the size of each square in a grid, I've included seam allowance to cut a square, half-square triangle, and quarter-square triangle. This is all the information you need to write instructions for or resize other blocks, or create your very own designs.

2 x 2 Grid
4 equal squares

		FINISHED BLOCK SIZE	6"	9"	12"
		GRID SQUARE SIZE	3 inch	4-1/2 inch	6 inch
add	1/2 inch	for square	3-1/2	5	6-1/2
add	7/8 inch	for HST	3-7/8	5-3/8	6-7/8
add	1-1/4 inch	for QST	4-1/4	5-3/4	7-1/4

3 x 3 Grid
9 equal squares

		FINISHED BLOCK SIZE	6"	9"	12"
		GRID SQUARE SIZE	2 inch	3 inch	4 inch
add	1/2 inch	for square	2-1/2	3-1/2	4-1/2
add	7/8 inch	for HST	2-7/8	3-7/8	4-7/8
add	1-1/4 inch	for QST	3-1/4	4-1/4	5-1/4

4 x 4 Grid
16 equal squares

		FINISHED BLOCK SIZE	6"	9"	12"
		GRID SQUARE SIZE	1-1/2 inch	2-1/4 inch	3 inch
add	1/2 inch	for square	2	2-3/4	3-1/2
add	7/8 inch	for HST	2-3/8	3-1/8	3-7/8
add	1-1/4 inch	for QST	2-3/4	3-1/2	4-1/4

6 x 6 Grid
36 equal squares

		FINISHED BLOCK SIZE	6"	9"	12"
		GRID SQUARE SIZE	1 inch	1-1/2 inch	2 inch
add	1/2 inch	for square	1-1/2	2	2-1/2
add	7/8 inch	for HST	1-7/8	2-3/8 inch	2-7/8
add	1-1/4 inch	for QST	2-1/4	2-3/4	3-1/4

INDEX

I am so grateful for my editorial friends at Landauer: Laurel Albright, Doris Brunnette, and Jeri Simon for their input, sewing skills and block designs. What a great team of women I am lucky enough to work with!

It was incredibly interesting and fun researching quilt blocks from books, (I have added several to my quilting library), and of course, the internet. The first of 201 blocks represented here are just the beginning for me. There are simply too many more I want to make and I'm motivated to continue designing my own.

And who knows? Maybe one of the blocks I design will still be good 100 years from now...